# KNITLYMPICS

First published in the United Kingdom in 2011 by
Collins & Brown
10 Southcombe Street
London
W14 0RA

An imprint of Anova Books Company Ltd

Distributed in the United States and Canada by
Sterling Publishing Co, 387 Park Avenue South,
New York, NY 10016-8810, USA

ISBN 978-1-84340-670-9

A CIP catalogue record for this book is available from
the British Library.

10 9 8 7 6 5 4 3 2 1

Reproduction by Rival Colour Ltd, UK
Printed and bound by G. Canale & C. S.p.A., Italy

This book can be ordered direct from the publisher at
www.anovabooks.com

# KNITLYMPICS

## KNIT YOUR FAVOURITE SPORTS STAR

**Carol Meldrum**

**COLLINS & BROWN**

# CONTENTS

# KNIT YOUR HERO

# THE ATHLETES

SEB COE

STEVE OVETT

6

# ON YOUR MARKS.....

As the date for the opening ceremony for the 2012 London Olympics approaches, the excitement is mounting. What better way to celebrate than through the versatile craft of knitting!

I have had so much fun trying to capture those wonderful moments of sporting glory and creating through knit the sporting heroes of the world. Looking back through the rich history of the Olympic Games, it was hard to choose the characters for this book but hopefully we have included some of the most iconic and recognisable athletes both past and present.

The book has been designed to be accessible to both beginner and experienced knitters. To help bring the characters and the Olympic spirit to life, each knitted athlete has a full set of instructions and all the knit, embroidery and craft techniques used to create those all-important details have been included at the back of the book.

It doesn't stop there, using the Basic Male and Basic Female doll patterns along with the appropriate basic clothing for the discipline in a different colour, you have everything you need to make your very own sporting hero. So why not knit those medals and the winner's podium in readiness?

There are also a few little extras for you to wear to help you celebrate and cheer on the athletes: a winner's wreath, a pair of wrist bands and the all-important and highly sought-after entrance ticket.

Get set, go – and let the Knitlympic Games begin!

*Carol Meldrum*

# KNITLYMPIC TICKET

## Size
21 x 11.5cm (8½ x 4⅝in)

## Materials
>>> Patons Fab DK; 68m/25g
ball (100% acrylic):
1 ball in white, 2306 (A)
1 ball in turquoise, 6343 (B)
1 ball in yellow, 2305 (C)
1 ball in black, 2311 (D)
1 ball in green, 2319 (E)
1 ball in red, 2323 (F)

>>> Anchor Artiste; 250m/
25g ball (65% Viscose,
35% Metallized Polyester):
1 ball in silver, 302 (G)
>>> Pair of 3.25mm (US 3)
knitting needles
>>> Pair of 2.75mm (US 2)
knitting needles
>>> Tapestry needle
>>> Bondaweb
20 x 11cm (8 x 4½in)
>>> Interfacing or white felt
fabric 20 x 11cm (8 x 4½in)

## Pattern
### TICKET BASE
Using A and 3.25mm (US 3)
needles, cast on 50 sts.
Rows 1–2: Knit.
Row 3: Knit.
Row 4: K2, p10, k2, p34, k2.
Repeat the last 2 rows 10 times
more.
Working in pattern set, join in
yarns B–F as required and break
off at the end stripe. Do not
break off yarn A.
Rows 23–24: Work using yarn B.
Row 25: Work using yarn A.
Repeat the last 3 rows 4 times
more; on each repeat, replace
yarn B with the following yarns
C, D, E, and F in turn.

Using yarn A only
Rows 37–38: Knit.
Cast off.

### SECURITY MONOGRAM
Using G and 2.75mm (US 2)
needles, cast on 10 sts.
Work 12 rows in stocking stitch.
Cast off.

## Finishing
Weave in ends and block ticket
base to a retangular shape.
Working from graph and using
the Swiss darning technique,
embroider KNIT TICKET on to
the larger section of the ticket.
Using backstitch, embroider
Admit 1 as shown.
Cut the Bondaweb and the
interfacing or white felt to fit
inside the outer garter stitch
border. With the wrong side of
ticket facing apply the
Bondaweb. Allow to cool then,
apply the interfacing or felt
fabric on top of the Bondaweb.
Use the Bondaweb to attach the
Security monogram.
As Bondaweb is an adhesive,
you will be able to cut off the
ticket stub with minimal fraying
of the fabric.

# KNITLYMPIC MEDALS

## Size
2cm (¾in) in diameter

## Materials
⟫⟫⟫ Anchor Artiste; 250m/
    25g ball (65% viscose,
    35% metallized polyester):
    1 ball in gold, 300 (A)
    1 ball in silver, 302 (B)
    1 ball in bronze, 314 (C)
⟫⟫⟫ Pair of 3.25mm (US 3)
    knitting needles
⟫⟫⟫ Tapestry needle
⟫⟫⟫ White ribbon or felt;
    8mm (⅜in) wide:
    25cm (10in) for each medal
⟫⟫⟫ Matching sewing thread
    and needle

## Pattern
### MEDAL
Using two strands of the correct colour for the medal worked together and 3.25mm (US 3) needles, cast on 8 sts.
Row 1 (WS): Purl.
Row 2: K2, [k2tog] twice, k2. (6 sts)
Break off yarn and thread through stitches on needle.
Draw tight and secure the end.

## Finishing
Weave in ends.
Using mattress stitch or backstitch, sew the side edges together to make a disc.
Fold the length of ribbon in half.
Place the ribbon ends, one on top of the other, at a 90-degree angle to each other.
Pin the ribbon to the back of the medal and stitch in position using sewing needle and thread.

# KNITLYMPIC RINGS

## Size
30 x 18cm (12 x 7in)

## Materials
》》》 Patons Fab DK; 68m/25g
    ball (100% acrylic):
    1 ball in yellow, 2305 (A)
    1 ball in green, 2319 (B)
    1 ball in red, 2323 (C)
    1 ball in black, 2311 (D)
    1 ball in turquoise, 6343 (E)
》》》 Two 4mm (US 6) double-
    pointed knitting needles
》》》 Tapestry needle
》》》 Craft wire
》》》 Small safety pin
》》》 Pair of pliers

## Pattern
### RINGS
Each ring is made from an i-cord.
Using A, 4mm (US 6) needles,
cast on 4 sts.
Row 1: Slide the 4 sts up to the
    right-hand point of needle,
    knit to end.
Repeat the last row until the
    work measures 30cm (12in)
    from the cast-on edge.
Cast off.
Repeat replacing A with B, and
    then with C, D and E.

## Finishing
Cut five lengths of craft wire
45cm (18in) long.
Using one wire length, fold over
the tip of one end to form a
loop, attach a small safety pin to
the loop and carefully thread
through the centre of the i-cord.
Repeat with each i-cord length.
Using the photograph as a
guide, link the split circles
together. Twist the two ends of
wire of each split circle to form a
complete circle approximately
10cm (4in) in diameter.

Use the pliers to flatten any
sharp edges.
To cover the wire, seam the two
open ends of the i-cord circle
together, using mattress stitch
or whipstitch.
To strengthen the structure,
stitch the knitted fabric of the
rings together at the points
where they interlock.

### FACT
The colours of the
rings were chosen in
1914 because at least
one of them featured
on the flag of every
country in the world.

# KNITLYMPIC TORCH

## Size
6 x 14cm (2½ x 5½in)

## Materials
>>> Patons Diploma Gold DK;
    120m/50g ball (55% wool,
    25% acrylic, 20% nylon):
    1 ball in grey, 6184 (MC)
>>> Pair of 3.25mm (US 3)
    knitting needles
>>> Tapestry needle
>>> Toy stuffing
>>> Felt fabric pieces;
    10 x 7.5cm (4 x 3in):
    1 in orange
    1 in yellow
    1 in red
    1 in black
>>> Matching sewing thread
    and needle

**FACT**
The Olympic flame is
a tradition continued
from the Ancient
Olympic Games.

## Pattern
**TORCH BASE**
Using MC and 3.25mm (US 3)
needles, cast on 38 sts.
Row 1: Knit.
Row 2: Knit.
Row 3: K5, k2tog, [k4, k2tog]
    5 times, k1. (32 sts)
Row 4: Knit.
Row 5: K4, k2tog, [k3, k2tog]
    5 times, k1. (26 sts)
Row 6: Knit.
Row 7: K3, k2tog, [k2, k2tog]
    5 times, k1. (20 sts)
Row 8: Knit.
Row 9: K2, k2tog, [k1, k2tog]
    5 times, k1. (14 sts)
Work 3 rows in stocking stitch.
Row 13: K1, [k2tog] 6 times, k1.
    (8 sts)
Work 4 rows in stocking stitch.
Break off yarn and thread
through stitches on needle.
Draw tight and secure the end.
Use same length to sew up the
side seam of torch.

## Finishing
Weave in ends.
Using mattress stitch or
backstitch, sew the side edges
together to make a cone.
Insert the toy stuffing into the
bottom of the cone.

Using the templates on page
95, cut out red, yellow and
orange flames from the felt.
Using the photograph as a
guide, arrange the flames and
stitch along the base of the felt
pieces to join them together.
To cover the stuffing inside the
torch, cut a circle from the black
felt approximately 2cm (¾in) in
diameter. Stitch the flames on to
the circle of black felt, then
stitch the black felt into the torch.

# KNITLYMPIC PODIUM

## Size
Bases approximately:
12.5cm (5in) square
Approximate heights: 4cm
(1½in); 5.5cm (2⅛in); 7.5cm (3in)

## Materials
>>> Sirdar Country Style;
318m/100g ball
(45% acrylic, 40% nylon,
15% wool):
1 ball in beige, 597 (MC)
>>> Pair of 3.75mm (US 5)
knitting needles
>>> Tapestry needle
>>> Three squares of thin card;
11 x 11cm (4½ x 4½in)
>>> Toy stuffing
>>> Felt fabric squares;
11 x 11cm (4½ x 4½in):
3 in brown
>>> Matching sewing thread
and needle

## Pattern
### BOTTOM OF BOX
### (MAKE 3)
Using MC and 3.75mm (US 5)
needles, cast on 25 sts.
Starting with a knit row, work
32 rows in stocking stitch.
Cast off.

### LARGE BOX SIDES
With WS facing, pick up 25 sts
evenly along cast-on edge of
the Bottom of box.
Starting with a knit row, work
24 rows in stocking stitch.
Cast off.
Repeat the above panel across
the cast-off edge and 2 sides.

### MEDIUM BOX SIDES
With WS facing, pick up 25 sts
evenly along cast-on edge of
the Bottom of box.
Starting with a knit row, work
18 rows in stocking stitch.
Cast off.
Repeat the above panel across
the cast-off edge and 2 sides.

### SMALL BOX SIDES
With WS facing, pick up 25 sts
evenly along cast-on edge of
the Bottom of the box.
Starting with a knit row, work
10 rows in stocking stitch.
Cast off.
Repeat the above panel across
the cast-off edge and 2 sides.

## Finishing
Weave in ends.
For each box, either sew up the
side seams with the WS facing
and using mattress stitch or with
RS facing and backstitch. This
will form a ridge on the right
side that helps give the box a
solid shape.
To further strengthen the box,
insert 11cm (4½in) square of thin
card into the Bottom of the box,
then insert stuffing, taking care
not to overstuff the box.
Pin a square of felt to the top of
the box. Using a sewing needle
and thread, stitch the felt square
to the top of the box.

### FACT
The first Modern Olympic
Games held under the
auspices of the International
Olympic Committee was
hosted in the Panathenaic
Stadium in Athens,
Greece, in 1896.

# KNITLYMPIC WREATH

## Size
To fit head circumference:
50cm (20in)

## Materials
- >>> Patons Fab DK; 68m/25g
  ball (100% acrylic):
  1 ball in green, 2319 (A)
- >>> Sirdar Country Style;
  318m/100g ball
  (45% acrylic, 40% nylon,
  15% wool):
  1 ball in mid-green, 595 (B)
- >>> Pair of 3.25mm (US 3)
  knitting needles
- >>> Tapestry needle
- >>> Wire coat hanger
- >>> Pair of wire cutters
- >>> Pair of pliers
- >>> Felt fabric square;
  30 x 30cm (12 x 12in):
  1 in green
- >>> Strip of brown felt fabric;
  60 x 1.5cm (24in x ½in)
- >>> Matching green sewing
  thread and needle

## Pattern
### LARGE KNITTED LEAF (MAKE 6)
Using A and 3.25mm (US 3)
needles, cast on 3 sts.
Row 1: Knit.
Row 2: Knit.

Row 3: [K1, yfwd] twice, k1. (5 sts)
Row 4: Knit.
Row 5: K2, yfwd, k1, yfwd, k2.
(7 sts)
Row 6: Knit.
Row 7: K3, yfwd, k1, yfwd, k3.
(9 sts)
Row 8: Knit.
Row 9: K3, yfwd, [k1, yfwd]
twice, k3. (13 sts)
Rows 10–16: Knit.
Row17: K4, ktogtbl, k1, k2tog,
k4. (11 sts)
Rows 18–20: Knit.

Row 21: K3, ktogtbl, k1, k2tog,
k3. (9 sts)
Row 22: Knit.
Row 23: K2, ktogtbl, k1, k2tog,
k2. (7 sts)
Rows 24–26: Knit.
Row 27: K1, ktogtbl, k1, k2tog,
k1. (5 sts)
Rows 28–30: Knit.
Row 31: K1, sl1, k2tog, psso, k1.
(3 sts)
Row 32: Knit.
Row 33: Sl1, k2tog, psso. (1 st)
Fasten off.

Perfect for watching
the Olympics in a
stadium or at home
with friends! Add
more felt leaves if you
don't want to make all
11 knitted leaves.

# WRIST BANDS

**SMALL KNITTED LEAF (MAKE 5)**
Using A and 3.25mm (US 3)
needles, cast on 3 sts.
Rows 1–6: Work as Large leaf
rows 1–6.
Row 7: K2, yfwd, [k1, yfwd]
twice, k2. (11 sts)
Rows 8–14: Knit.
Rows 15–27: Work as Large leaf
rows 21–33. Fasten off.

## Finishing
Weave in ends.
**Felt leaves**
Using leaf template on page 95,
cut 12 leaf shapes from the
green felt fabric.
**Wreath base**
Using wire cutters, cut the head
off the coat hanger, to create a
single length of wire. Using
pliers, twist the wire into a circle
that will sit comfortably on top
of the head. Twist the two ends
of the wire together to form a
circle. Use the pliers to flatten
any sharp edges. Wrap the strip
of brown felt around the wire
and stitch in place.
Using the photograph as guide,
pin and stitch the felt and
knitted leaves on to the Wreath
base in a crisscross pattern.

## Size
To fit wrist circumference:
16cm (6¼in)
Depth: 9cm (3½in)

## Materials
>>> Patons Fab DK; 68m/25g
ball (100% acrylic):
1 ball in yellow, 2305 (A)
1 ball in green, 2319 (B)
1 ball in red, 2323 (C)
1 ball in black, 2311 (D)
1 ball in turquoise, 6343 (E)
>>> Pair of 3.25mm (US 3)
knitting needles
>>> Tapestry needle

## Tension
22 sts x 40 rows = 10cm (4in)
square over garter stitch using
3.25mm (US 3) needles.

## Note
The wrist bands can be made
wider by adding more rows to
the stripes.
To make the wristband deeper,
cast on more stitches.

## Pattern
**WRIST BAND (MAKE 2)**
Using A and 3.25mm (US 3)
needles, cast on 20 sts.

Rows 1–6: Using A, knit.
Rows 7–12: Using B, knit.
Rows 13–18: Using C, knit.
Rows 19–24: Using D, knit.
Rows 25–30: Using E, knit.
Repeat rows 1–30 once more.
Cast off.

## Finishing
Weave in ends.
Fold in half, cast-on edge to
cast-off edge, and using
mattress stitch or whip stitch,
sew the edges together.

# BASIC MALE DOLL

## Size
Approximate height: 33cm (13in)

## Materials
》》》 DK-weight yarn specified by the doll pattern
》》》 Pair of 3.25mm (US 3) knitting needles
》》》 Tapestry needle
》》》 Toy stuffing

## Tension
25 sts x 34 rows = 10cm (4in) square over stocking stitch using 3.25mm (US 3) needles.

This basic doll pattern is used for all the male dolls in this book. A specific materials list and additional information can be found on the pattern pages of each character.

## Pattern
**BODY AND HEAD**

Cast on 28 sts.

Row 1 (WS): Purl.

Row 2 (RS): K6, m1, k2, m1, k12, m1, k2, m1, k6. (32 sts)

Row 3: Purl.

Row 4: K7, m1, k2, m1, k14, m1, k2, m1, k7. (36 sts)

Work 5 rows in stocking stitch.

Row 10: K6, k2tog, k2, k2togtbl, k12, k2tog, k2, k2togtbl, k6. (32 sts)

Row 11: Purl.

Row 12: K5, k2tog, k2, k2togtbl, k10, k2tog, k2, k2togtbl, k5. (28 sts)

Work 5 rows in stocking stitch.

Row 18: K6, m1, k2, m1, k12, m1, k2, m1, k6. (32 sts)

Row 19: Purl.

Row 20: K7, m1, k2, m1, k14, m1, k2, m1, k7. (36 sts)

Work 3 rows in stocking stitch.

Row 24: K8, m1, k2, m1, k16, m1, k2, m1, k8. (40 sts)

Work 7 rows in stocking stitch.

Row 32: K7, k2tog, k2, k2togtbl, k14, k2tog, k2, k2togtbl, k7. (36 sts)

Row 33: P6, p2togtbl, p2, p2tog, p12, p2togtbl, p2, p2tog, p6. (32 sts)

Row 34: K5, k2tog, k2, k2togtbl, k10, k2tog, k2, k2togtbl, k5. (28 sts)

Row 35: P4, p2togtbl, p2, p2tog, p8, p2togtbl, p2, p2tog, p4. (24 sts)

Row 36: K3, k2tog, k2, k3togtbl, k4, k3tog, k3, k2togtbl, k3. (18 sts)

Work 3 rows in stocking stitch

### Head

Row 40 (RS): K4, m1, k2, m1, k6, m1, k2, m1, k4. (22 sts)

Row 41: P5, m1, p2, m1, p8, m1, p2, m1, p5. (26 sts)

Row 42: K6, m1, k2, m1, k10, m1, k2, m1, k6. (30 sts)

Work 11 rows in stocking stitch.

Row 54: K5, k2tog, k2, k2togtbl, k8, k2tog, k2, k2togtbl, k5. (26 sts)

Row 55: P4, p2togtbl, p2, p2tog, p6, p2togtbl, p2, p2tog, p4. (22 sts)

Row 56: K3, k2tog, k2, k2togtbl, k4, k2tog, k2, k2togtbl, k3.

Cast off.

### ARMS (MAKE 2)

Cast on 12 sts.

Starting with a knit row, work 32 rows in stocking stitch.

Row 33: K1, [k2tog] twice, k2, [k2tog] twice, k1. (8 sts)

Row 34: Purl.

Row 35: K2, [m1, k2] 3 times. (11 sts)

Row 36: Purl.

Row 37: K2, m1, k3, m1, k4, m1, k2. (14 sts)

Work 7 rows in stocking stitch.

Row 45: K1, [k2tog] 6 times, k1. (8 sts)

Break off yarn and thread through stitches on needle. Draw tight and secure the end.

### LEGS (MAKE 2)

Cast on 15 sts.

Starting with a knit row, work 4 rows in stocking stitch.

Row 5: K4, k2tog, k3, k2tog, k4. (13 sts)

Work 33 rows in stocking stitch.

### Shape feet

Row 39: K1, m1, k5, m1, k1, m1, k5, m1, k1. (17 sts)

Row 40: Purl.

Row 41: K8, m1, k1, m1, k8. (19 sts)

Row 42: Purl.

Row 43: K9, m1, k1, m1, k7, turn, do not work remaining sts on the left-hand needle.

Row 44: Sl1, p16, turn.

Row 45: Sl1, k7, m1, k1, m1, k6, turn.

Row 46: Sl1, p14, turn.

Row 47: Sl1, k6, m1, k1, m1, k3, turn.

Row 48: Sl1, p8, turn.

Row 49: Sl1, knit to end of row.

Cast off knitwise.

## Finishing

Weave in ends.

Gently press pieces.

### Body and head

Using mattress stitch or backstitch, sew the side edges together to form the back seam. Sew together the edges on the top of the Head. Insert stuffing and sew the bottom seam.

### Neck

Using a length of yarn without an end knot, insert the tapestry needle at back seam, just under the first row of increasing for head. Weave the needle in and out of stitches around neck, pull tight and tie a double knot, then sew in the loose ends.

### Arms

Sew the side edges together to create the back seam. Insert stuffing and sew up the top opening. Using the same method as that described for the Neck, add wrists 3cm (1⅛in) from the fastened-off stitches. Using the decrease stitches on the shoulders as a guide, attach the arms to the Body.

### Legs

Fold the cast-off edge in half, then sew together the cast-off edge and back seam. Insert stuffing and sew up the top opening. Attach the legs to the Body.

# BASIC FEMALE DOLL

## Size
Approximate height:
27cm (10½in)

## Materials
>>> DK-weight yarn specified by the doll pattern
>>> Pair of 3.25mm (US 3) knitting needles
>>> Tapestry needle
>>> Toy stuffing

## Tension
25 sts x 34 rows = 10cm (4in) square over stocking stitch using 3.25mm (US 3) needles.

## Pattern
**BODY AND HEAD**
Cast on 28 sts.
Row 1 (WS): Purl.
Row 2 (RS): K6, m1, k2, m1, k12, m1, k2, m1, k6. (32 sts)
Row 3: Purl.
Row 4: K7, m1, k2, m1, k14, m1, k2, m1, k7. (36 sts)
Work 5 rows in stocking stitch.
Row 10: K6, k2tog, k2, k2togtbl, k12, k2tog, k2, k2togtbl, k6. (32 sts)
Row 11: Purl.

Row 12: K5, k2tog, k2, k2togtbl, k10, k2tog, k2, k2togtbl, k5. (28 sts)
Work 5 rows in stocking stitch.
Row 18: K6, m1, k2, m1, k12, m1, k2, m1, k6. (32 sts)
Work 3 rows in stocking stitch.
Row 22: K7, m1, k2, m1, k14, m1, k2, m1, k7. (36 sts)

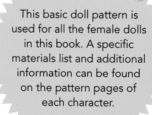

This basic doll pattern is used for all the female dolls in this book. A specific materials list and additional information can be found on the pattern pages of each character.

18

Work 7 rows in stocking stitch.
Row 30: K6, k2tog, k2, k2togtbl, k12, k2tog, k2, k2togtbl, k6. (32 sts)
Row 31: P5, p2togtbl, p2, p2tog, p10, p2togtbl, p2, p2tog, p5. (28 sts)
Row 32: K4, k2tog, k2, k2togtbl, k8, k2tog, k2, k2togtbl, k4. (24 sts)
Row 33: P3, p2togtbl, p2, p3tog, p4, p3togtbl, p2, p2tog, p3. (18 sts)
Work 4 rows in stocking stitch.

### Head
Row 38 (RS): K4, m1, k2, m1, k6, m1, k2, m1, k4. (22 sts)
Row 39: P5, m1, p2, m1, p8, m1, p2, m1, p5. (26 sts)
Row 40: K6, m1, k2, m1, k10, m1, k2, m1, k6. (30 sts)
Work 9 rows in stocking stitch.
Row 50: K5, k2tog, k2, k2togtbl, k8, k2tog, k2, k2togtbl, k5. (26 sts)
Row 51: P4, p2togtbl, p2, p2tog, p6, p2togtbl, p2, p2tog, p4. (22 sts)
Row 52: K3, k2tog, k2, k2togtbl, k4, k2tog, k2, k2togtbl, k3. (18 sts)
Cast off.

### ARMS (MAKE 2)
Cast on 10 sts.
Starting with a knit row, work 28 rows in stocking stitch.

Row 29: K1, [k2tog] 4 times, k1. (6 sts)
Row 30: Purl.
Row 31: K1, [m1, k2] twice, m1, k1. (9 sts)
Work 7 rows in stocking stitch.
Row 39: K1, [k3tog, k1] twice, k1. (5 sts)
Break off yarn and thread through stitches on needle. Draw tight and secure the end.

### LEGS (MAKE 2)
Cast on 13 sts.
Starting with a knit row, work 34 rows in stocking stitch.
### Shape feet
Row 35: K1, m1, k5, m1, k1, m1, k5, m1, k1. (17 sts)
Row 36: Purl.
Row 37: K8, m1, k1, m1, k8. (19 sts)
Row 38: Purl.
Row 39: K9, m1, k1, m1, k7, turn, do not work remaining sts on the left-hand needle.
Row 40: Sl1, p16, turn.
Row 41: Sl1, k7, m1, k1, m1, k6, turn.
Row 42: Sl1, p14, turn.
Row 43: Sl1, k6, m1, k1, m1, k3, turn.
Row 44: Sl1, p8, turn.
Row 45: Sl1, knit to end of row.
Cast off knitwise.

## Finishing
Weave in ends.
Gently press pieces.
### Body and head
Using mattress stitch or backstitch, sew the side edges together to form the back seam. Sew together the edges on the top of the Head. Insert stuffing and sew the bottom seam.
### Neck
Using a length of yarn without an end knot, insert the tapestry needle at back seam, just under the first row of increasing for head. Weave the needle in and out of stitches around neck, pull tight and tie a double knot, then sew in the loose ends.
### Arms
Sew the side edges together to create the back seam. Insert stuffing and sew up the top opening. Using the same method as that described for the Neck, add wrists 2cm (¾in) from the fastened-off stitches. Using the decrease stitches on the shoulders as a guide, attach the arms to the Body.
### Legs
Fold the cast-off edge in half, then sew together the cast-off edge and back seam. Insert stuffing and sew up the top opening. Attach the legs to the Body.

# KNIT YOUR HERO!

There are so many Olympic heroes and heroines and too little space to celebrate them all!

To avoid disappointment, the following patterns have been selected to enable you to construct your own favourite Olympic icon. Study the doll patterns in the book for ideas on how to achieve the distinctive sport-clothing style.

All the following basic outfits will fit both the Basic Male Doll on page 16 and the Basic Female Doll on page 17, except the leotard which will only fit the Basic Female Doll.

# BASIC ALL-IN-ONE SUIT

## Materials
>>> DK-weight yarn such as Patons Fab DK; 68m/25g ball (100% acrylic):
1 ball in main colour, (MC)
1 ball in contrast colour, (CC)
>>> Pair of 3.25mm (US 3) knitting needles
>>> Stitch holder
>>> Tapestry needle

## Tension
25 sts x 34 rows = 10cm (4in) square over stocking stitch using 3.25mm (US 3) needles.

## Note
To work in a single colour, skip the intarsia instructions.

## Pattern
### ALL-IN-ONE SUIT
**Legs (make 2)**
Using MC and 3.25mm (US 3) needles, cast on 20 sts.
Row 1: Knit.
Row 2: Purl.
Side stripes are worked using the intarsia technique. Keep the foll colour st patt correct throughout. Join in CC.
Row 3: K7MC, k6CC, k7MC.
Work 5 rows in stocking stitch.
Transfer on to a stitch holder and make Leg 2.
**Join legs**
Row 9: Knit 20 sts on Leg 1, knit across 20 sts on Leg 2. (40 sts)
Row 10: Purl.
Work 6 rows in stocking stitch.
Row 17: K7, k2tog, k2, k2togtbl, k14, k2togtbl, k2, k2tog, k7. (36 sts)
Work 3 rows in stocking stitch.
Row 21: K7, k2tog, k2togtbl, k14, k2togtbl, k2tog, k7. (32 sts)
Work 3 rows in stocking stitch.
Row 25: K8, m1, k2, m1, k16, m1, k2, m1, k8. (36 sts)
Work 9 rows in stocking stitch.
Row 35: K7, cast off 4 sts, k14 (include the last st from cast-off in the count), cast off 4 sts, k7 (include the last st from cast-off in the count).
Transfer the first 21 sts of the last row on to a stitch holder.

### Shape back right neck
Work 2 rows in stocking stitch.
Row 38: Cast off 2 sts, purl to
   last st, k1. (5 sts)
Row 39: K1, k2tog, k1. (4 sts)
Row 40: K1, p2tog, k1. (3 sts)
Row 41: Knit.
Row 42: K1, p1, k1.
Cast off.

### Shape back left neck
Transfer the group of 7 sts from
   stitch holder on to the needle
   and rejoin yarn with WS facing.
Work 2 rows in stocking stitch.
Row 38: Cast off 2 sts, purl to
   end. (5 sts)
Row 39: K1, k2togtbl, k1. (4 sts)
Row 40: K1, p2togtbl, k1. (3 sts)
Row 41: Knit.
Row 42: K1, p1, k1.
Cast off.

### Shape front neck
Transfer 14 sts from stitch
   holder on to the needle and
   rejoin yarn with WS facing.
Work 2 rows in stocking stitch.
Row 38: K1, purl to last st, k1.
Row 39: K4, p1, transfer the
   remaining 9 sts on to a stitch
   holder or safety pin. (5 sts)

### Shape front left neck
Row 40 (WS): K1, p3, k1.
Row 41: K2, k2tog, k1. (4 sts)
Row 42: K1, p2, k1.
Row 43: K1, k2tog, k1. (3 sts)
Row 44: K1, p1, k1.
Cast off.

### Shape front right neck
Transfer 9 sts from stitch
   holder on to the needle
   and rejoin yarn with
   RS facing.
Row 39: Cast off 4 sts, knit
   to end. (5 sts)
Row 40 (WS): K1, p3, k1.
Row 41: K1, k2togtbl, k2.
   (4 sts)
Row 42: K1, p2, k1,
Row 43: K1, k2togtbl, k1. (3 sts)
Row 44: K1, p1, k1.
Cast off.

## Finishing
Weave in ends.
Using mattress stitch or
backstitch, sew the side edges
together to create the leg
seams and a back seam.
Dress doll in the suit and sew
shoulder seams.

# BASIC LEOTARD

## Materials

>>> DK-weight yarn such as Patons Fab DK; 68m/25g ball (100% acrylic): 1 ball in main colour, (MC)
>>> Pair of 3.25mm (US 3) knitting needles
>>> Stitch holder or safety pin
>>> Tapestry needle

## Tension

25 sts x 34 rows = 10cm (4in) square over stocking stitch using 3.25mm (US 3) needles.

## Pattern

### LEOTARD FRONT

Using MC and 3.25mm (US 3) needles, cast on 14 sts.
Row 1 (WS): Purl.

Row 2: K1, m1, knit to last st, m1, k1. (16 sts)
Row 3: Purl.
Row 4: K1, m1, knit to last st, m1, k1. (18 sts)
Work 5 rows in stocking stitch.
Row 10: K1, k2togtbl, knit to last 3 sts, k2tog, k1. (16 sts)
Row 11: Purl.
Row 12: K1, k2togtbl, knit to last 3 sts, k2tog, k1. (14 sts)
Work 5 rows in stocking stitch.
Row 18: K1, m1, knit to last st, m1, k1. (16 sts)
Row 19: Purl.**

Shape top
Row 20: K1, m1, k7, transfer the rem 8 sts on to a stitch holder or safety pin. (9 sts)
Work 3 rows in stocking stitch.
Row 24: K1, k2togtbl, k3, k2tog, k1. (7 sts)
Row 25: Purl.
Row 26: K1, k2togtbl, k1, k2tog, k1. (5 sts)
Row 27: Purl.
Row 28: K1, sl1, k2tog, psso, k1. (3 sts)
Row 29: Purl.
Cast off.
Transfer 8 sts from stitch holder on to the needle and rejoin yarn with RS facing.

Row 20: K7, m1, k1. (9 sts)
Work 3 rows in stocking stitch.
Row 24: K1, k2togtbl, k3, k2tog,
    k1. (7 sts)
Row 25: Purl.
Row 26: K1, k2togtbl, k1, k2tog,
    k1. (5 sts)
Row 27: Purl.
Row 28: K1, sl1, k2tog, psso, k1.
    (3 sts)
Row 29: Purl.
Cast off.

## LEOTARD BACK

Using MC and 3.25mm (US 3)
needles, cast on 14 sts.
Work as given for front until **.
Shape top
Row 20: K1, m1, knit to last st,
    m1, k1. (18 sts)
Work 3 rows in stocking stitch.
Row 24: K1, k2togtbl, knit to last
    3 sts, k2tog, k1. (16 sts)
Row 25: Purl.
Repeat last 2 rows twice more.
    (12 sts)
Cast off.

## SLEEVES (MAKE 2)

Using MC and 3.25mm (US 3)
needles, cast on 13 sts.
Starting with a knit row, work
22 rows in stocking stitch.

Shape top
Row 23: K1, k2togtbl, knit to last
    3 sts, k2tog, k1. (11 sts)
Row 24: P1, p2tog, purl to last
    3 sts, p2togtbl, p1. (9 sts)
Repeat last 2 rows once more.
    (5 sts)
Row 27: K1, sl1, k2tog, psso, k1.
    (3 sts)
Row 28: P3tog.
Fasten off.

## Finishing

Weave in ends.
Using mattress stitch or
backstitch, sew the side edges
of the two pieces together to
create side seams, sew shoulder
seams and sew in sleeves.
Dress the doll in the Leotard
and stitch the centre 3 stitches
on cast-on edges together to
create leg holes.

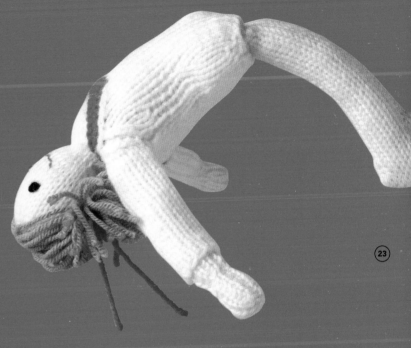

# BASIC TRAINERS

## Materials

>>> DK-weight yarn such as Patons Fab DK; 68m/25g ball (100% acrylic): 1 ball in main colour, (MC)

>>> Short length of contrast yarn

>>> Pair of 3.25mm (US 3) knitting needles

>>> Tapestry needle

## Tension

25 sts x 34 rows = 10cm (4in) square over stocking stitch using 3.25mm (US 3) needles.

## Pattern

**TRAINERS (MAKE 2)**

Using MC and 3.25mm (US 3) needles, cast on 17 sts.

Row 1: Purl.

Row 2: K1, m1, k6, m1, k3, m1, k6, m1, k1. (21 sts)

Row 3: Purl.

Row 4: K9, m1, k3, m1, k9. (23 sts)

Row 5: Purl.

**Shape toe**

Row 6: K10, m1, k3, m1, k8, turn, do not work remaining sts on the left-hand needle.

Row 7: Sl1, p20, turn.

Row 8: Sl1, k8, m1, k3, m1, k7, turn.

Row 9: Sl1, p18, turn.

Row 10: Sl1, k7, m1, k3, m1, k6, turn.

Row 11: Sl1, p16, turn.

Row 12: Sl1, knit to end.

Row 13: P12, p2tog, p1, p2tog, p12. (27 sts)

Cast off.

## Finishing

Weave in ends.

Fold the cast-off edge in half, then sew together the cast-off edge and back seam.

For laces, cut a length of contrast yarn, thread it through the top of the trainers and tie it into a bow.

**Tip**

For more information on how to embellish a pair of trainers, see the Cathy Freeman doll on page 67 or the Michael Johnson doll on page 70.

# BASIC VEST

## Materials

- DK-weight yarn such as Patons Fab DK; 68m/25g ball (100% acrylic):
  1 ball in main colour, (MC)
  1 ball in white, 2306 (CC)
- Short length of black yarn
- Pair of 3.25mm (US 3) knitting needles
- Stitch holder or safety pin
- Tapestry needle

## Tension

25 sts x 34 rows = 10cm (4in) square over stocking stitch using 3.25mm (US 3) needles.

## Pattern

**VEST (MAKE 2)**

Using MC and 3.25mm (US 3) needles, cast on 20 sts.
Row 1: Knit.
Row 2: Knit.
Starting with a knit row, work 20 rows in stocking stitch.
Cast off 2 sts at beginning of next 2 rows. (16 sts)
Work 2 rows in stocking stitch.

**Shape neck**

Row 25 (RS): K4, p1, transfer the rem 11 sts on to a stitch holder or safety pin. (5 sts)
Row 26: K1, p4.

Row 27: K2, k2tog, k1. (4 sts)
Row 28: K1, p3.
Row 29: K1, k2tog, k1. (3 sts)
Row 30: K1, p2.
Cast off.
Transfer 11 sts from stitch holder on to the needle and rejoin yarn.
Row 25: Cast off 6 sts, knit to end. (5 sts)
Row 26: P4, k1.
Row 27: K1, k2togtbl, k2. (4 sts)
Row 28: P3, k1,
Row 29: K1, k2togtbl, k1. (3 sts)
Row 30: P2, k1.
Cast off.

**NUMBER PANEL**

Using CC and 3.25mm (US 3) needles, cast on 10 sts.
Row 1: Knit.
Row 2: K1, p8, k1.
Repeat last 2 rows 3 times more.
Cast off.

## Finishing

Weave in ends.
Using mattress stitch or backstitch, sew the side edges of the two pieces together to create side seams and sew shoulder seams.
Using a short length of black yarn and backstitch, embroider a number on to the Number Panel, and pin and stitch it to the front of the Vest.

# DISCOBOLUS

## Materials

**DOLL**
- Patons Diploma Gold DK; 120m/50g ball (55% wool, 25% acrylic, 20% nylon): 1 ball in grey, 6184 (MC)
- Pair of 3.25mm (US 3) knitting needles
- Pair of 3.75mm (US 5) knitting needles
- Stitch holder
- Toy stuffing
- Tapestry needle

**OUTFIT**
- Sirdar Bonus DK; 280m/ 100g ball (100% acrylic): 1 ball in grey, 837 (CC)

- Felt fabric circles; 6cm (2½in) in diameter: 2 in grey
- One circle of thin card; 5cm (2in) in diameter
- Matching grey sewing thread and needle
- Safety pin

## Pattern

**DOLL**
Using MC, make a Basic Male Doll following the instructions on page 16.

**EARS (MAKE 2)**
Using MC and 3.25mm (US 3) needles, cast on 6 sts.
Row 1: Knit.
Break off yarn and thread through stitches on needle.
Draw tight and secure the end.

**HAIR**
Using MC and 3.25mm (US 3) needles, cast on 6 sts.
Work 4 rows in garter stitch.
Cast on 4 sts at beginning of next 2 rows. (14 sts)
Work 4 rows in garter stitch.
Cast off 2 sts at beginning of next 2 rows. (10 sts)
Work 10 rows in garter stitch.

Next row: K1, sl1, k2tog, psso, knit to last 4 sts, k3tog, k1. (6 sts)
Cast off knitwise.

**TOGA (OPTIONAL)**
Using CC and 3.75mm (US 5) needles, cast on 20 sts.
Rows 1–2: Knit.
Row 3: K2, purl to last 2 sts, k2.
Row 4: Purl.
Repeat last 2 rows 3 times more.
Work 16 rows in stocking stitch.
Row 27: K1, m1, knit to last st, m1, k1. (22 sts)
Row 28: Purl.
Row 29: Repeat row 27. (24 sts)
Row 30: P1, m1, purl to last st, m1, p1. (26 sts)
Row 31: Repeat row 27. (28 sts)
Row 32: Repeat row 30. (30 sts)
Work 9 rows in stocking stitch.
Row 42: K10, cast off 10 sts, knit to end. (20 sts)
Row 43: K10, cast on 10 sts, knit to end. (30 sts)
Work 6 rows in stocking stitch.
Row 50: P1, p2tog, purl to last 3 sts, p2togtbl, p1. (28 sts)
Row 51: K1, k2togtbl, knit to last 3 sts, k2tog, k1. (26 sts)
Row 52: Repeat row 50. (24 sts)
Row 53: Repeat row 51. (22 sts)

Row 54: Purl.
Row 55: Repeat row 51.
  (20 sts)
Work 13 rows in stocking stitch.
Row 69: K2, purl to last 2 sts, k2.
Row 70: Knit.
Repeat last 2 rows 3 times more.
Rows 77–78: Knit.
Cast off knitwise.

## Finishing
Use the photographs as a guide
throughout the finishing of
the pieces and use matching
yarn unless otherwise stated.
Weave in ends using the seams
where appropriate.
Assemble the doll as given for
the finishing of the Basic Male
Doll on page 17.
**Head and face**
Pin and stitch hair and ears to
the head.

The original
Olympian... an
ancient Greek
discus thrower!

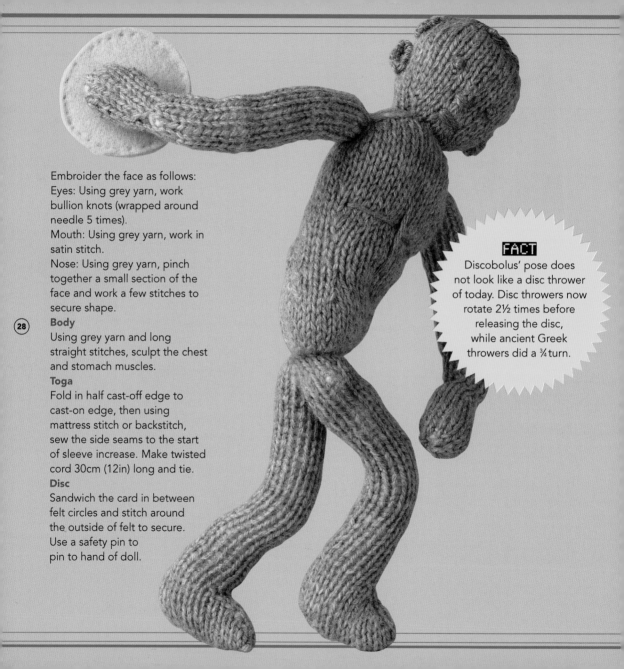

Embroider the face as follows:
Eyes: Using grey yarn, work bullion knots (wrapped around needle 5 times).
Mouth: Using grey yarn, work in satin stitch.
Nose: Using grey yarn, pinch together a small section of the face and work a few stitches to secure shape.

**Body**
Using grey yarn and long straight stitches, sculpt the chest and stomach muscles.

**Toga**
Fold in half cast-off edge to cast-on edge, then using mattress stitch or backstitch, sew the side seams to the start of sleeve increase. Make twisted cord 30cm (12in) long and tie.

**Disc**
Sandwich the card in between felt circles and stitch around the outside of felt to secure. Use a safety pin to pin to hand of doll.

**FACT**
Discobolus' pose does not look like a disc thrower of today. Disc throwers now rotate 2½ times before releasing the disc, while ancient Greek throwers did a ¾ turn.

# JESSE OWENS

## FACT FILE

**SPORT**
Athletics (100m, 200m, 4 x 100m relay, long jump)

**NICKNAME**
The Buckeye Bullet

**DOB**
12 September, 1913
(D. 31 March, 1980)

**NATIONALITY**
American

**OLYMPIC MEDALS**
4 Gold (1936, Berlin)

## Materials

**DOLL**
>>> Patons Fab DK; 274m/100g ball (100% acrylic):
   1 ball in brown, 2309 (A)
>>> Patons Fab DK; 68m/25g ball (100% acrylic):
   1 ball in black, 2311 (B)
>>> Pair of 3.25mm (US 3) knitting needles
>>> Stitch holder or safety pin
>>> Toy stuffing
>>> Tapestry needle

**OUTFIT**
>>> Patons Fab DK; 68m/25g ball (100% acrylic):
   1 ball in white, 2306 (C)
>>> Short length of red yarn
>>> Short length of navy blue yarn

## Pattern

**DOLL**
Using A, make a Basic Male Doll following the instructions on page 16.

**EARS (MAKE 2)**
Using A and 3.25mm (US 3) needles, cast on 6 sts.
Row 1: Knit.
Break off yarn and thread through stitches on needle. Draw tight and secure the end.

**HAIR**
Using B and 3.25mm (US 3) needles, cast on 4 sts.
Work 10 rows in garter stitch.
Next row: K1, m1, k2, m1, k1.
   (6 sts)
Continue working in garter stitch until the strip fits from top of head to back of neck.
Cast off.

## VEST (MAKE 2)

Using C and 3.25mm (US 3) needles, cast on 20 sts.

Row 1: Knit.

Row 2: Knit.

Starting with a knit row, work 20 rows in stocking stitch.

Rows 23–24: Cast off 2 sts at the beginning of row. (16 sts)

Rows 25–26: Work 2 rows in stocking stitch.

### Shape neck

Row 27 (RS): K4, p1, transfer the rem 11 sts on to a stitch holder or safety pin. (5 sts)

Row 28: K1, p4.

Row 29: K2, k2tog, k1. (4 sts)

Row 30: K1, p3.

Row 31: K1, k2tog, k1. (3 sts)

Row 32: K1, p2.

Cast off.

Transfer 11 sts from stitch holder on to the needle, rejoin yarn.

Row 27: Cast off 6 sts, knit to end. (5 sts)

Row 28: P4, k1.

Row 29: K1, k2togtbl, k2. (4 sts)

Row 30: P3, k1.

Row 31: K1, k2togtbl, k1. (3 sts)

Row 32: P2, k1.

Cast off.

## SHORTS

### Legs (make 2)

Using C and 3.25mm (US 3) needles, cast on 18 sts.

Row 1: Knit.

Row 2: Knit.

Starting with a knit row, work 6 rows in stocking stitch.

Transfer on to a stitch holder and make Leg 2.

### Join legs

Row 9: Knit 18 sts on Leg 1, knit across 18 sts on Leg 2. (36 sts)

Row 10: Purl.

Work 9 rows in stocking stitch.

Row 20: Knit.

Row 21: K2, [k2tog, yfwd, k2] 4 times, k2, [k2tog, yfwd, k2] 3 times, k2tog, yfwd, k2.

Cast off knitwise.

## TRAINERS (MAKE 2)

Using C and 3.25mm (US 3) needles, cast on 17 sts.

Row 1: Purl.

Row 2: K1, m1, k6, m1, k3, m1, k6, m1, k1. (21 sts)

Row 3: Purl.

Row 4: K9, m1, k3, m1, k9. (23 sts)

Row 5: Purl.

### Shape toe

Row 6: K10, m1, k3, m1, k8, turn, do not work remaining sts on the left-hand needle.

Row 7: Sl1, p20, turn.

Row 8: Sl1, k8, m1, k3, m1, k7, turn.

Row 9: Sl1, p18, turn.

Row 10: Sl1, k7, m1, k3, m1, k6, turn.

Row 11: Sl1, p16, turn.

Row 12: Sl1, knit to end.

Row 13: P12, p2tog, p1, p2tog, p12. (27 sts)

Cast off.

## Finishing

Use the photographs as a guide throughout the finishing of the pieces and use matching yarn unless otherwise stated. Weave in ends using the seams where appropriate.

Assemble the doll as given for the finishing of the Basic Male Doll on page 17.

### Head and face

Pin and stitch hair and ears to the head.

Using black yarn, work French knots around the edge of the strip of hair and on top of the head to create the hairline.

Embroider the face as follows:

Eyes: Using black yarn, work bullion knots (wrapped around needle 5 times).

Mouth: Using black yarn, work one long straight stitch.

### Vest

Using mattress stitch or backstitch, sew the side edges of the two pieces together to create side seams and sew shoulder seams.

Using backstitch, embroider red and navy diagonal lines across the front.

### Shorts

Using mattress stitch or backstitch, sew the side edges together to create the back leg seams.

Using white yarn, make twisted cord 30cm (12in) long and thread through the eyelets.

### Trainers

Fold the cast-off edge in half, then sew together the cast-off edge and back seam.

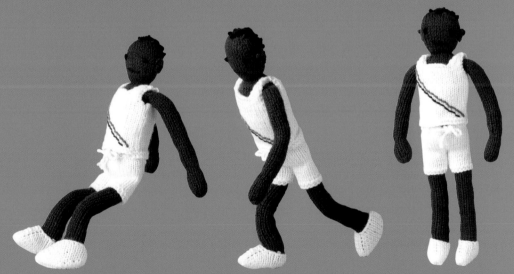

# FRANCINA
# BLANKERS-KOEN

★★★★★★★★★★★★★★★★★
### FACT FILE
**SPORT**
Athletics (100m, 200m,
80m hurdles, 4 x 100m relay)
**NICKNAME**
The Flying Housewife
**DOB**
26 April, 1918
(D. 25 January, 2004)
**NATIONALITY**
Dutch
**OLYMPIC MEDALS**
4 Gold (1948, London)
★★★★★★★★★★★★★★★★★

## Materials
**DOLL**
>>> Patons Fab DK; 274m/100g
ball (100% acrylic):
1 ball in cream, 2307 (A)
>>> Patons Diploma Gold DK;
120m/50g ball (55% wool,
25% acrylic, 20% nylon):
1 ball in beige, 6143 (B)
>>> Pair of 3.25mm (US 3)
knitting needles
>>> One 2.75mm (C–2)
crochet hook
>>> Stitch holder or safety pin
>>> Toy stuffing
>>> Tapestry needle
>>> Red embroidery thread
>>> Embroidery needle

**OUTFIT**
>>> Adriafil Azzura; 225m/50g
ball (30% wool/30% acrylic):
1 ball in orange, 34 (C)
>>> Patons Fab DK; 68m/25g
ball (100% acrylic):
1 ball in white, 2306 (D)
1 ball in black, 2311 (E)

## Pattern
**DOLL**
Using A, make a Basic Female
Doll following the instructions
on page 18.

**SHIRT FRONT**
Using D and 3.25mm (US 3)
needles, cast on 14 sts.
Rows 1–2: Knit.
Starting with a knit row, work
4 rows in stocking stitch.
Row 7: K1, m1, knit to last st,
m1, k1. (16 sts)
Row 8: Purl.
Work 8 rows in stocking stitch.
**Shape neck**
Row 17: K1, m1, k7, transfer the
rem 8 sts on to a stitch holder
or safety pin. (9 sts)
Row 18: K2, p7.
Row 19: K1, m1, knit to end.
(10 sts)
Row 20: K2, p8.
Row 21: K1, m1, knit to end.
(11 sts)
Row 22: K2, p9.
Row 23: Knit.
Row 24: K3, purl to end.
Row 25: Cast off 3 sts, k to end.

Row 26: K3, purl to end.
Cast off.
Transfer stitches from stitch holder and rejoin yarn.
Row 17: Knit to last st, m1, k1. (9 sts)
Row 18: P7, k2.
Row 19: K to last st, m1, k1. (10 sts)
Row 20: P8, k2.
Row 21: K to last st, m1, k1. (11 sts)
Row 22: P8, k3.
Row 23: Knit.
Row 24: Cast off 3 sts, purl to last 3 sts, k3.
Row 25: Knit.
Cast off.

## SHIRT BACK

Using D and 3.25mm (US 3) needles, cast on 14 sts.
Work as Shirt Front until **.
### Shape neck
Row 17: K1, m1, knit to last st, m1, k1. (18 sts)
Row 18: Purl.
Repeat last 2 rows twice more. (22 sts)
Work 2 rows in stocking stitch.
Cast off 3 sts at the beginning of next 2 rows.
Cast off.

## NUMBER PANEL

Using D and 3.25mm (US 3) needles, cast on 10 sts.

Row 1: Knit.
Row 2: K1, p8, k1.
Repeat last 2 rows 3 times more.
Cast off.

## SHORTS
### Leg (make 2)
Using C and 3.25mm (US 3) needles, cast on 24 sts.
Rows 1–2: Knit.
Starting with a knit row, work 4 rows in stocking stitch.
Row 7: K5, sl1, k2tog, psso, k8, sl1, k2tog, psso, knit to end. (20 sts)
Row 8: Purl.
Transfer on to a stitch holder and make Leg 2.
Row 9: Knit 20 sts on Leg 1, knit across 20 sts on Leg 2. (40 sts)
Starting with a purl row, work 10 rows in stocking stitch.

Next row (WS): Knit.
Next row: K1, [k2tog, yfwd, k3] 7 times, k2tog, yfwd, k2.
Cast off knitwise.

## TRAINERS (MAKE 2)
Using E and 3.25mm (US 3) needles, cast on 17 sts.
Row 1: Purl.

**FACT**
Blankers-Koen's most prized possession was Jesse Owens' signature from the 1936 Games.

Row 2: K1, m1, k6, m1, k3, m1, k6, m1, k1. (21 sts)
Row 3: Purl.
Row 4: K9, m1, k3, m1, k9. (23 sts)
Row 5: Purl.

Shape toe
Next row: K10, m1, k3, m1, k8, turn, do not work remaining sts on the left-hand needle.
Next row: Sl1, p20, turn.
Next row: Sl1, k8, m1, k3, m1, k7, turn.
Next row: Sl1, p18, turn.
Next row: Sl1, k7, m1, k3, m1, k6, turn.
Next row: Sl1, p16, turn.
Next row: Sl1, knit to end.
Next row: P12, p2tog, p1, p2tog, p12. (27 sts)
Cast off.

# Finishing

Use the photographs as a guide throughout the finishing of the pieces and use matching yarn unless otherwise stated. Weave in ends using the seams where appropriate.
Assemble the doll as given for the finishing of the Basic Female Doll on page 19.

Hair
Using yarn B, cut 18 lengths of yarn 30cm (12in) long and divide the lengths into 6 sections of 3 yarn lengths. Attach the hair to the head along the top seam by inserting a crochet hook under a stitch, folding a section of hair in half and pulling it through the fabric to form a loop, then pass the cut ends of strands through the loop and pull tight to form a tassel. Attach one more line of hair lengths, slightly offset and immediately behind the first. Draw the hair to the back of the head and work a loose plait. To secure the end of the plait, cut a length of beige yarn and tie into a bow.

Face
Embroider the face as follows:
Eyes: Using black yarn, work bullion knots (wrapped around needle 5 times).
Mouth: Using red embroidery thread, work in backstitch.

Shirt
Using mattress stitch or backstitch, sew the shoulder and side seams.
Fold back garter stitch collar at front and stitch down.
Using a short length of black yarn and backstitch, embroider a number on to the Number Panel, then pin and stitch it to the front of the Shirt.

Shorts
Using mattress stitch or backstitch, sew the side edges together to create the back leg seams.

Using orange yarn, make twisted cord 30cm (12in) long and thread through the eyelets.

Trainers
Fold the cast-off edge in half, then sew together the cast-off edge and back seam.
For laces, cut a length of white yarn and, using straight stitch, embroider the top of the trainers.

# EMIL ZATOPEK

## Materials

**DOLL**
>>> Patons Fab DK; 274m/100g
ball (100% acrylic):
1 ball in cream, 2307 (A)
>>> Patons Diploma Gold DK;
120m/50g ball (55% wool,
25% acrylic, 20% nylon):
1 ball in beige, 6143 (B)
>>> Pair of 3.25mm (US 3)
knitting needles
>>> Stitch holder or safety pin
>>> Tapestry needle
>>> Toy stuffing
>>> Red embroidery thread
>>> Embroidery needle

**OUTFIT**
>>> Patons Fab DK; 68m/25g
ball (100% acrylic):
1 ball in red, 2306 (C)
1 ball in white, 2306 (D)
1 ball in black, 2311 (E)

## Pattern

**DOLL**
Using A, make a Basic Male Doll
following the instructions on
page 16.

## HAIR
Using B and 3.25mm (US 3)
needles, cast on 6 sts.
Work 4 rows in garter stitch.
Cast on 4 sts at beginning of
next 2 rows. (14 sts)
Work 4 rows in garter stitch.
Cast off 2 sts at beginning of
next 2 rows. (10 sts)
Work 10 rows in garter stitch.
Next row: K1, sl1, k2tog, psso,
knit to last 4 sts, k3tog, k1.
(6 sts)
Cast off knitwise.

## VEST (MAKE 2)
Using C and 3.25mm (US 3)
needles, cast on 20 sts.
Row 1: Knit.
Row 2: Knit.
Starting with a knit row, work
20 rows in stocking stitch.
Rows 23–24: Cast off 2 sts at the
beginning of row. (16 sts)
Rows 25–26: Work 2 rows in
stocking stitch.
**Shape neck**
Row 27 (RS): K4, p1, transfer the
rem 11 sts on to a stitch
holder or safety pin. (5 sts)
Row 28: K1, p4.
Row 29: K2, k2tog, k1. (4 sts)
Row 30: K1, p3.

Row 31: K1, k2tog, k1. (3 sts)
Row 32: K1, p2.
Cast off.
Transfer 11 sts from stitch holder
    on to the needle and rejoin
    yarn.
Row 27: Cast off 6 sts, knit to
    end. (5 sts)
Row 28: P4, k1.
Row 29: K1, k2togtbl, k2. (4 sts)
Row 30: P3, k1.
Row 31: K1, k2togtbl, k1. (3 sts)
Row 32: P2, k1.
Cast off.

### NUMBER PANEL

Using D and 3.25mm (US 3)
needles, cast on 10 sts.
Row 1: Knit.
Row 2: K1, p8, k1.
Repeat last 2 rows 3 times more.
Cast off.

### SHORTS

**Legs (make 2)**
Using D and 3.25mm (US 3)
needles, cast on 18 sts.
Row 1: Knit.
Row 2: Knit.
Starting with a knit row, work
    6 rows in stocking stitch.
Transfer on to a stitch holder
    and make Leg 2.
**Join legs**
Row 9: Knit 18 sts on Leg 1, knit
    across 18 sts on Leg 2. (36 sts)
Row 10: Purl.

Work 9 rows in stocking stitch.
Row 20: Knit
Row 21: K2, [k2tog, yfwd, k2]
    4 times, k2, [k2tog, yfwd, k2]
    3 times, k2tog, yfwd, k2.
Cast off knitwise.

### TRAINERS (MAKE 2)

Using E and 3.25mm (US 3)
needles, cast on 17 sts.
Row 1: Purl.
Row 2: K1, m1, k6, m1, k3, m1,
    k6, m1, k1. (21 sts)
Row 3: Purl.
Row 4: K9, m1, k3, m1, k9. (23 sts)
Row 5: Purl.
**Shape toe**
Next row: K10, m1, k3, m1, k8,
    turn, do not work remaining
    sts on the left-hand needle.
Next row: Sl1, p20, turn.
Next row: Sl1, k8, m1, k3, m1,
    k7, turn.
Next row: Sl1, p18, turn.
Next row: Sl1, k7, m1, k3, m1,
    k6, turn.
Next row: Sl1, p16, turn.
Next row: Sl1, knit to end.
Next row: P12, p2tog, p1,
    p2tog, p12. (27 sts)
Cast off.

## Finishing

Use the photographs as a guide
throughout the finishing of
the pieces and use matching
yarn unless otherwise stated.

'If you want to run, run a mile. If you want to experience a different life, run a marathon.'

**FACT**
Zatopek was the first athlete to break the 29-minute time barrier for 10km in 1954.

Weave in ends using the seams where appropriate.
Assemble the doll as given for the finishing of the Basic Male Doll on page 17.

**Head and face**
Pin and stitch hair to the head.
Embroider the face as follows:
Eyes: Using black yarn, work bullion knots (wrapped around needle 5 times).
Mouth: Using red embroidery thread, work in backstitch.

**Vest**
Using mattress stitch or backstitch, sew the side edges of the two pieces together to create side seams and sew shoulder seams.

Using a short length of black yarn and backstitch, embroider a number on to the Number Panel, then pin and stitch it to the front of the Vest.

**Shorts**
Using mattress stitch or backstitch, sew the side edges together to create the back leg seams.
Using white yarn, make twisted cord 30cm (12in) long and thread through the eyelets.

**Trainers**
Fold the cast-off edge in half, then sew together the cast-off edge and back seam.
For laces, cut a length of white yarn, thread through the top of the trainers and tie into a bow.

# RICHARD FOSBURY

## Materials

**DOLL**

》》》 Patons Fab DK; 274m/100g ball (100% acrylic): 1 ball in cream, 2307 (A)
》》》 Patons Fab DK; 68m/25g ball (100% acrylic): 1 ball in brown, 2309 (B)
》》》 Pair of 3.25mm (US 3) knitting needles
》》》 Stitch holder or safety pin
》》》 Tapestry needle
》》》 Toy stuffing
》》》 Short length of black yarn
》》》 Red embroidery thread
》》》 Embroidery needle

**OUTFIT**

》》》 Patons Diploma Gold DK; 120m/50g ball (55% wool, 25% acrylic, 20% nylon): 1 ball in navy blue, 6167 (C)
》》》 Patons Fab DK; 274m/100g ball (100% acrylic): 1 ball in white, 2306 (D)
》》》 Short length of red yarn

## Pattern

**DOLL**

Using A, make a Basic Male Doll following the instructions on page 16.

**HAIR**

Using B and 3.25mm (US 3) needles, cast on 13 sts.
Rows 1–6: Knit.
Row 7: K1, m1, knit to last st, m1, k1. (15 sts)
Row 8: Knit.
Row 9: Work as row 7. (17 sts)
Rows 10–20: Knit.
Row 21: K4, k2togtbl, k5, k2tog, k4. (15 sts)
Row 22: Knit.
Row 23: K4, k2togtbl, k3, k2tog, k4. (13 sts)
Row 24: Knit.
Row 25: K4, k2togtbl, k1, k2tog, k4. (11 sts)
Work 3 rows in garter stitch.
Row 29: K1, k2togtbl, knit to last 3 sts, k2tog, k1. (9 sts)
Rows 30–33: Knit.
Cast off.

**VEST (MAKE 2)**

Using C and 3.25mm (US 3) needles, cast on 20 sts.
Row 1: Knit.
Row 2: Knit.
Starting with a knit row, work 20 rows in stocking stitch.
Rows 23–24: Cast off 2 sts at the beginning of row. (16 sts)

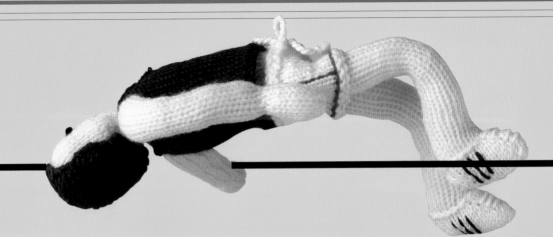

Rows 25–26: Work 2 rows in stocking stitch.

**Shape neck**

Row 27 (RS): K4, p1, transfer the rem 11 sts on to a stitch holder or safety pin. (5 sts)

Row 28: K1, p4.

Row 29: K2, k2tog, k1. (4 sts)

Row 30: K1, p3.

Row 31: K1, k2tog, k1. (3 sts)

Row 32: K1, p2.

Cast off.

Transfer 11 sts from stitch holder on to the needle and rejoin yarn.

Row 27: Cast off 6 sts, knit to end. (5 sts)

Row 28: P4, k1.

Row 29: K1, k2togtbl, k2. (4 sts)

Row 30: P3, k1.

Row 31: K1, k2togtbl, k1. (3 sts)

Row 32: P2, k1.

Cast off.

## SHORTS

### Legs (make 2)

Using D and 3.25mm (US 3) needles, cast on 18 sts.

Row 1: Knit.

Row 2: Knit.

Starting with a knit row, work 4 rows in stocking stitch.

Transfer on to a stitch holder and make Leg 2.

### Join legs

Row 7: Knit 18 sts on Leg 1, knit across 18 sts on Leg 2. (36 sts)

Row 8: Purl.

Work 9 rows in stocking stitch.

Row 18: Knit.

Row 19: K2, [k2tog, yfwd, k2] 4 times, k2, [k2tog, yfwd, k2] 3 times, k2tog, yfwd, k2.

Cast off knitwise.

## TRAINERS (MAKE 2)

Using D and 3.25mm (US 3) needles, cast on 17 sts.

Row 1: Purl.

Row 2: K1, m1, k6, m1, k3, m1, k6, m1, k1. (21 sts)

Row 3: Purl.

Row 4: K9, m1, k3, m1, k9. (23 sts)

Row 5: Purl.

**Shape toe**

Next row: K10, m1, k3, m1, k8, turn, do not work remaining sts on the left-hand needle.

Next row: Sl1, p20, turn.

Next row: Sl1, k8, m1, k3, m1, k7, turn.

Next row: Sl1, p18, turn.

Next row: Sl1, k7, m1, k3, m1, k6, turn.

Next row: Sl1, p16, turn.

Next row: Sl1, knit to end.

Next row: P12, p2tog, p1, p2tog, p12. (27 sts)

Cast off.

## Finishing

Use the photographs as a guide throughout the finishing of the pieces and use matching yarn unless otherwise stated. Weave in ends using the seams where appropriate.

Assemble the doll as given for the finishing of the Basic Male Doll on page 17.

### Head and face

Pin and stitch hair to the head. Embroider the face as follows:
Eyes: Using black yarn, work bullion knots (wrapped around needle 5 times).
Mouth: Using red embroidery thread, work in backstitch.

### Vest

Using mattress stitch or backstitch, sew the side edges of the two pieces together to create side seams and sew shoulder seams.

### Shorts

Using mattress stitch or backstitch, sew the side edges together to create the back leg seams.

Using red yarn and backstitch, embroider along bottom edge of shorts and vertically up each outer leg.

Using white yarn, make twisted cord 30cm (12in) long and thread through the eyelets.

### Trainers

Fold the cast-off edge in half, then sew together the cast-off edge and back seam.

Using navy blue yarn and backstitch, embroider three vertical lines on the inside and outside of each trainer.

### FACT
Fosbury was the first person to go over the high jump bar head first, with a leap that is now called the 'Fosbury Flop'.

# MARK SPITZ

## Materials
**DOLL**
>>> Patons Fab DK; 274m/100g
ball (100% acrylic):
1 ball in cream, 2307 (A)
>>> Patons Diploma Gold DK;
120m/50g ball (55% wool,
25% acrylic, 20% nylon):
1 ball in beige, 6143 (B)
>>> Pair of 3.25mm (US 3)
knitting needles
>>> Stitch holder or safety pin
>>> Tapestry needle
>>> Toy stuffing
>>> Short length of black yarn

**OUTFIT**
>>> Patons Diploma Gold DK;
120m/50g ball (55% wool,
25% acrylic, 20% nylon):
1 ball in navy blue, 6167 (C)
>>> Oddment of red yarn
>>> Oddment of white yarn

## Pattern
**DOLL**
Using A, make a Basic Male Doll
following the instructions on
page 16.

**HAIR**
Using B and 3.25mm (US 3)
needles, cast on 13 sts.

Rows 1–6: Knit.
Row 7: K1, m1, knit to
last st, m1, k1. (15 sts)
Row 8: Knit.
Row 9: Repeat row 7.
(17 sts)
Rows 10–20: Knit.
Row 21: K4, k2togtbl,
k5, k2tog, k4. (15 sts)
Row 22: Knit.
Row 23: K4, k2togtbl, k3,
k2tog, k4. (13 sts)
Row 24: Knit.
Row 25: K4, k2togtbl, k1,
k2tog, k4. (11 sts)

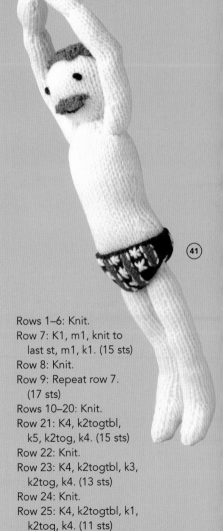

Rows 26–28: Knit.
Row 29: K1, k2togtbl, knit to last
  3 sts, k2tog, k1. (9 sts)
Rows 30–32: Knit.
Row 33: K1, k2togtbl, k to last
  3 sts, k2tog, k1.
Cast off.

## MOUSTACHE
Using B and 3.25mm (US 3)
needles, cast on 13 sts.
Row 1: K1, sl1, k2tog, psso, knit
  to end.
Row 2: Cast off 4 sts, k3tog,
  pso, cast off to end.

## TRUNKS
Worked from top down.
Using B and 3.25mm (US 3)
needles, cast on 40 sts.
Starting with a knit row, work
  6 rows in stocking stitch.
Row 7: K8, cast off 4 sts, k16,
  cast off 4 sts, knit to end.
  (8 sts; 16 sts; 8 sts)

Work each of these sections
separately as follows:

**First 8-stitch section**

Row 1 (WS): Purl to last 3 sts,
p2tog, k1. (7 sts)

Row 2: K1, k2tog, knit to end.
(6 sts)

Row 3: Work as row 1. (5 sts)

Row 4: Work as row 2. (4 sts)

Row 5: P2, k1.

Row 6: Knit.

Cast off.

Rejoin yarn to next set of 16 sts.

**16-stitch section**

Row 1 (WS): K1, p2togtbl,
purl to last 3 sts, p2tog, k1.
(14 sts)

Row 2: K1, k2tog, knit to last
3 sts, k2togtbl, k1. (12 sts)

Row 3: Work as row 1. (10 sts)

Row 4: Work as row 2. (8 sts)

Row 5: Work as row 1. (6 sts)

Row 6: Work as row 2. (4 sts)

Cast off.

**Last 8-stitch section**

Row 1 (WS): P1, p2togtbl, purl
to end. (7 sts)

Row 2: Knit to last 3 sts, sl1, k1,
psso, k1. (6 sts)

Row 3: Work as row 1. (5 sts)

Row 4: Work as row 2. (4 sts)

Row 5: K1, p2.

Row 6: Knit.

Cast off.

## Finishing

Use the photographs as a guide
throughout the finishing of
the pieces and use matching
yarn unless otherwise stated.
Weave in ends using the seams
where appropriate.

Assemble the doll as given for
the finishing of the Basic Male
Doll on page 17.

**Head and face**

Pin and stitch hair and
moustache to the head.
Embroider the face as follows:
Eyes: Using black yarn, work
bullion knots (wrapped around
needle 5 times).
Mouth: Using black yarn, work
two long straight stitches.

**Trunks**

Using mattress stitch or
backstitch, sew back seam of
trunks together and then sew
the cast-off stitches from front
and back to form leg openings.
Using red yarn and leaving two
stitches between each of the
vertical stripes, work columns of
Swiss darning. Using white yarn,
work a line of backstitch down
either side of the red stripe,
then work stars on the blue
background.

(43)

**FACT**

Spitz called his
signature moustache
his 'good-luck piece',
but he shaved it off
when it began to
grow grey hairs.

# OLGA KORBUT

## Materials

**DOLL**

>>> Patons Fab DK; 274m/100g
ball (100% acrylic):
1 ball in cream, 2307 (A)
>>> Patons Diploma Gold DK;
120m/50g ball (55% wool,
25% acrylic, 20% nylon):
1 ball in beige, 6143 (B)
>>> Pair of 3.25mm (US 3)
knitting needles
>>> One 2.75mm (C–2)
crochet hook
>>> Stitch holder or safety pin
>>> Toy stuffing
>>> Tapestry needle
>>> Short length of black yarn
>>> Red embroidery thread
>>> Embroidery needle

**OUTFIT**

>>> Patons Fab DK; 68m/25g
ball (100% acrylic):
1 ball in white, 2306 (C)
1 ball in red, 2306 (D)

## Pattern

**DOLL**

Using A, make a Basic Female
Doll following the instructions
on page 18.

**LEOTARD FRONT**

Using C and 3.25mm (US 3)
needles, cast on 14 sts.
Row 1 (WS): Purl.
Row 2: K1, m1, knit to last st,
m1, k1. (16 sts)
Row 3: Purl.
Row 4: K1, m1, knit to last st,
m1, k1. (18 sts)
Work 5 rows in stocking stitch.
Row 10: K1, k2togtbl, knit to last
3 sts, k2tog, k1. (16 sts)
Row 11: Purl.
Row 12: K1, k2togtbl, knit to last
3 sts, k2tog, k1. (14 sts)
Work 5 rows in stocking stitch.
Row 18: K1, m1, knit to last st,
m1, k1. (16 sts)
Row 19: Purl.**
Shape top
Row 20: K1, m1, k7, transfer the
rem 8 sts on to a stitch holder
or safety pin. (9 sts)
Work 3 rows in stocking stitch.
Row 24: K1, k2togtbl, k3, k2tog,
k1. (7 sts)
Row 25: Purl.
Row 26: K1, k2togtbl, k1, k2tog,
k1. (5 sts)
Row 27: Purl.
Row 28: K1, sl1, k2tog, psso, k1.
(3 sts)
Row 29: Purl.

**FACT**
Korbut is famous for two moves, the 'Korbut Flip' and the 'Korbut Salto'.

Cast off.
Transfer 8 sts from stitch holder on to the needle and rejoin yarn with RS facing.
Row 20: K7, m1, k1. (9 sts)
Work 3 rows in stocking stitch.
Row 24: K1, k2togtbl, k3, k2tog, k1. (7 sts)
Row 25: Purl.
Row 26: K1, k2togtbl, k1, k2tog, k1. (5 sts)
Row 27: Purl.
Row 28: K1, sl1, k2tog, psso, k1. (3 sts)
Row 29: Purl.
Cast off.

## LEOTARD BACK
Using C and 3.25mm (US 3) needles, cast on 14 sts.
Work as given for front until **.
### Shape top
Row 20: K1, m1, knit to last st, m1, k1. (18 sts)
Work 3 rows in stocking stitch.
Row 24: K1, k2togtbl, knit to last 3 sts, k2tog, k1. (16 sts)
Row 25: Purl.
Repeat last 2 rows twice more. (12 sts)
Cast off.

## SLEEVES (MAKE 2)
Using C and 3.25mm (US 3) needles, cast on 13 sts.
Starting with a knit row, work 22 rows in stocking stitch.
### Shape top
Row 23: K1, k2togtbl, knit to last 3 sts, k2tog, k1. (11 sts)
Row 24: P1, p2tog, purl to last 3 sts, p2togtbl, p1. (9 sts)
Repeat last 2 rows once more. (5 sts)
Row 27: K1, sl1, k2tog, psso, k1. (3 sts)
Row 28: P3tog.
Fasten off.

## Finishing
Use the photographs as a guide throughout the finishing of the pieces and use matching yarn unless otherwise stated. Weave in ends using the seams where appropriate.
Assemble the doll as given for the finishing of the Basic Female Doll on page 19.
### Hair
Using yarn B, cut 36 lengths of yarn 30cm (12in) long and divide the lengths into 12 sections of 3 yarn lengths. To create a centre parting, attach the hair to the

head along the centre of the head by inserting a crochet hook under a stitch, folding a section of hair in half and pulling it through the fabric to form a loop, then pass the cut ends of strands through the loop and pull tight to form a tassel. Draw the hair into two bunches on either side of the head and secure with lengths of red yarn tied into bows.

## Face

Embroider the face as follows:

Eyes: Using black yarn, work bullion knots (wrapped around needle 5 times).

Mouth: Using red embroidery thread, work in backstitch.

## Leotard

Using mattress stitch or backstitch, sew the doll's right shoulder seam.

Using yarn D and with right side facing, pick up sts along neck line using 3.25mm (US 3) needle as follows: 11 sts down left side of neck, place marker, 11 sts up right side of neck, 6 sts along back of neck, leaving 3 sts at end for other shoulder. (28 sts)

Row 1: Knit to last 2 sts before the marker, k2tog, slip marker, k2tog, knit to end. (26 sts)

Repeat last row once more (24 sts)

Cast off knitwise.

Using mattress stitch or backstitch, sew the left shoulder and neckband together, sew the side edges of the two pieces together to create side seams and sew in sleeves.

Dress the doll in the Leotard and stitch the centre 3 stitches on cast-on edges together to create leg holes.

**FACT**
After the 1972 Olympics, Korbut returned home to piles of fan mail.

# NADIA COMANECI

## Materials
**DOLL**
>>> Patons Fab DK; 274m/100g
ball (100% acrylic):
1 ball in brown, 2309 (A)
>>> Patons Fab DK; 68m/25g
ball (100% acrylic):
1 ball in dark brown,
2309 (B)
>>> Pair of 3.25mm (US 3)
knitting needles
>>> Stitch holder or
safety pin
>>> Tapestry needle
>>> Toy stuffing
>>> One 2.75mm (C–2)
crochet hook

>>> White ribbon;
8mm (⅜in) wide:
30cm (12in) for hair bunch
>>> Short length of black yarn
>>> Red embroidery thread
>>> Embroidery needle

**OUTFIT**
>>> Patons Fab DK; 68m/25g
ball (100% acrylic):
1 ball in white, 2306 (C)
1 ball in yellow, 2305 (D)
>>> Small amount of blue yarn
>>> Small amount of red yarn

## Pattern
**DOLL**
Using A, make a Basic Female
Doll following the instructions
on page 18.

**LEOTARD FRONT**
Using MC and 3.25mm (US 3)
needles, cast on 14 sts.
Row 1 (WS): Purl.
Row 2: K1, m1, knit to last st,
m1, k1. (16 sts)
Row 3: Purl.

(47)

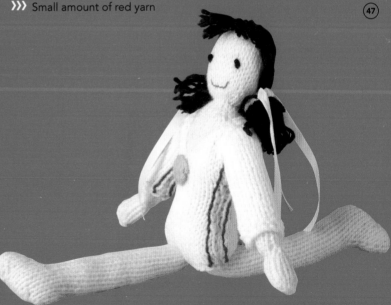

Row 4: K1, m1, knit to last st, m1, k1. (18 sts)
Work 5 rows in stocking stitch.
Row 10: K1, k2togtbl, knit to last 3 sts, k2tog, k1. (16 sts)
Row 11: Purl.
Row 12: K1, k2togtbl, knit to last 3 sts, k2tog, k1. (14 sts)
Work 5 rows in stocking stitch.
Row 18: K1, m1, knit to last st, m1, k1. (16 sts)
Row 19: Purl.**

Shape top
Row 20: K1, m1, k7, transfer the rem 8 sts on to a stitch holder or safety pin. (9 sts)
Work 3 rows in stocking stitch.
Row 24: K1, k2togtbl, k3, k2tog, k1. (7 sts)
Row 25: Purl.
Row 26: K1, k2togtbl, k1, k2tog, k1. (5 sts)
Row 27: Purl.
Row 28: K1, sl1, k2tog, psso, k1. (3 sts)
Row 29: Purl.
Cast off.
Transfer 8 sts from stitch holder on to the needle and rejoin yarn with RS facing.
Row 20: K7, m1, k1. (9 sts)
Work 3 rows in stocking stitch.
Row 24: K1, k2togtbl, k3, k2tog, k1. (7 sts)
Row 25: Purl.
Row 26: K1, k2togtbl, k1, k2tog, k1. (5 sts)

Row 27: Purl.
Row 28: K1, sl1, k2tog, psso, k1. (3 sts)
Row 29: Purl.
Cast off.

## LEOTARD BACK
Using MC and 3.25mm (US 3) needles, cast on 14 sts.
Work as given for front until **.
Shape top
Row 20: K1, m1, knit to last st, m1, k1. (18 sts)
Work 3 rows in stocking stitch.
Row 24: K1, k2togtbl, knit to last 3 sts, k2tog, k1. (16 sts)
Row 25: Purl.
Repeat last 2 rows twice more. (12 sts)
Cast off.

## SLEEVES (MAKE 2)
Using MC and 3.25mm (US 3) needles, cast on 13 sts.
Starting with a knit row, work 22 rows in stocking stitch.
Shape top
Row 23: K1, k2togtbl, knit to last 3 sts, k2tog, k1. (11 sts)
Row 24: P1, p2tog, purl to last 3 sts, p2togtbl, p1. (9 sts)
Repeat last 2 rows once more. (5 sts)
Row 27: K1, sl1, k2tog, psso, k1. (3 sts)
Row 28: P3tog.
Fasten off.

## FRONT MOTIF
Using D and 3.25mm (US 3) needles, cast on 8 sts.
Row 1: Purl.
Row 2: K1, [k2tog] 3 times, k1. (5 sts)
Break off yarn and thread through stitches on needle. Draw tight and sew the side edges together to make a disc.

# Finishing
Use the photographs as a guide throughout the finishing of the pieces and use matching yarn unless otherwise stated. Weave in ends using the seams where appropriate.
Assemble the doll as given for the finishing of the Basic Female Doll on page 19.
Hair
Using yarn B, cut 48 lengths of yarn 30cm (12in) long and divide the lengths into 16 sections of 3 yarn lengths. To create a centre parting, attach the hair to the head along the centre of the head by inserting a crochet hook under a stitch, folding a section of hair in half and pulling it through the fabric to form a loop, then pass the cut ends of strands through the loop and pull tight to form a tassel.
For the fringe, attach two lengths of hair either side of

centre parting, cut short, spray
with water and pin into position.
Leave to dry before removing
pins. Draw the hair into two
bunches on either side of the
head and secure with lengths of
white ribbon tied into bows.

**Face**

Embroider the face as follows:
Eyes: Using black yarn, work
bullion knots (wrapped around
needle 5 times).
Mouth: Using red embroidery
thread, work in backstitch.

**Leotard**

Using mattress stitch or
backstitch, sew the side edges
of the two pieces together to
create side seams, sew shoulder
seams and sew in sleeves.
Using backstitch, embroider
vertical lines in blue, red and
yellow next to the side seams
and down the sleeve seam.
Stitch motif into position at
centre of front.
Dress the doll in the Leotard
and stitch the centre 3 stitches
on cast-on edges together to
create leg holes.

**FACT**

Comaneci is
married to gold medal
winning American
gymnast Bart
Conner.

# STEVE OVETT

## Materials

**DOLL**
- ⟫⟫ Patons Fab DK; 274m/100g ball (100% acrylic): 1 ball in cream, 2307 (A)
- ⟫⟫ Patons Fab DK; 68m/25g ball (100% acrylic): 1 ball in dark brown, 2309 (B)
- ⟫⟫ Pair of 3.25mm (US 3) knitting needles
- ⟫⟫ Stitch holder or safety pin
- ⟫⟫ Tapestry needle
- ⟫⟫ Toy stuffing
- ⟫⟫ Short length of black yarn
- ⟫⟫ Red embroidery thread
- ⟫⟫ Embroidery needle

**OUTFIT**
- ⟫⟫ Patons Fab DK; 68m/25g ball (100% acrylic): 1 ball in white, 2306 (C)
- ⟫⟫ Patons Diploma Gold DK; 120m/50g ball (55% wool, 25% acrylic, 20% nylon): 1 ball in navy, 6167 (D)
- ⟫⟫ Patons Fab DK; as above: 1 ball in red, 2306 (E)

## Pattern

**DOLL**
Using A, make a Basic Male Doll following the instructions on page 16.

**EARS (MAKE 2)**
Using A and 3.25mm (US 3) needles, cast on 6 sts.
Row 1: Knit.
Break off yarn and thread through stitches on needle. Draw tight and secure the end.

**HAIR**
Using B and 3.25mm (US 3) needles, cast on 6 sts.
Work 4 rows in garter stitch.
Cast on 4 sts at beginning of next 2 rows. (14 sts)
Work 4 rows in garter stitch.
Cast off 2 sts at beginning of next 2 rows. (10 sts)
Work 10 rows in garter stitch.
Next row: K1, sl1, k2tog, psso, knit to last 4 sts, k3tog, k1. (6 sts)
Cast off knitwise.

**VEST (MAKE 2)**
Using C and 3.25mm (US 3) needles, cast on 20 sts.
Row 1: Knit.
Row 2: Knit.
Starting with a knit row, work 9 rows in stocking stitch.
Break off C, join in D.
Work 3 rows in stocking stitch.
Break off D, join in C.
Row 15: Purl.
Break off C, join in E.
Work 3 rows in stocking stitch.
Break off E, join in C.
Work 2 rows in stocking stitch.
Rows 21–22: Cast off 2 sts at beginning of row. (16 sts)
Row 23: Knit.
Row 24: Purl.
**Shape neck**
Row 25 (RS): K4, p1, transfer the rem 6 sts on to a stitch holder or safety pin. (5 sts)
Row 26: K1, p4.
Row 27: K2, k2tog, k1. (4 sts)
Row 28: K1, p3.

Row 29: K1, k2tog, k1. (3 sts)
Row 30: K1, p2.
Cast off.
Transfer stitches from stitch
    holder on to the needle and
    rejoin yarn.
Row 25: Cast off 6 sts, knit to
    end. (5 sts)
Row 26: P4, k1.
Row 27: K1, k2togtbl, k2. (4 sts)
Row 28: P3, k1.
Row 29: K1, k2togtbl, k1. (3 sts)
Row 30: P2, k1.
Cast off.

## NUMBER PANEL

Using D and 3.25mm (US 3)
needles, cast on 10 sts.
Row 1: Knit.
Row 2: K1, p8, k1.
Repeat last 2 rows 3 times more.
Cast off.

## SHORTS
### Legs (make 2)
Using D and 3.25mm (US 3)
needles, cast on 18 sts.
Row 1: Knit.
Row 2: Knit.
Starting with a knit row, work
    6 rows in stocking stitch.
Transfer on to a stitch holder
    and make Leg 2.
### Join legs
Row 9: Knit 18 sts on Leg 1, knit
    across 18 sts on Leg 2. (36 sts)
Row 10: Purl.

Work 9 rows in stocking
    stitch.
Row 20: Knit
Row 21: K2 [k2tog, yfwd,
    k2] 4 times, k2, [k2tog,
    yfwd, k2] 3 times, k2tog,
    yfwd, k2.
Cast off knitwise.

## TRAINERS (MAKE 2)
Using C and 3.25mm
(US 3) needles, cast on 17 sts.
Row 1: Purl.
Row 2: K1, m1, k6, m1, k3,
    m1, k6, m1, k1. (21 sts)
Row 3: Purl.
Row 4: K9, m1, k3, m1, k9.
    (23 sts)
Row 5: Purl.
### Shape toe
Next row: K10, m1, k3,
    m1, k8, turn, do not
    work remaining sts on
    the left-hand needle.
Next row: Sl1, p20, turn.
Next row: Sl1, k8, m1, k3, m1,
    k7, turn.
Next row: Sl1, p18, turn.
Next row: Sl1, k7, m1, k3, m1,
    k6, turn.
Next row: Sl1, p16, turn.
Next row: Sl1, knit to end.
Next row: P12, p2tog, p1,
    p2tog, p12. (27 sts)
Cast off.

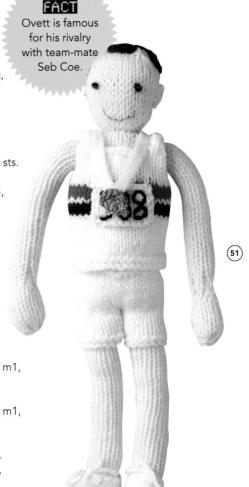

**FACT**
Ovett is famous
for his rivalry
with team-mate
Seb Coe.

51

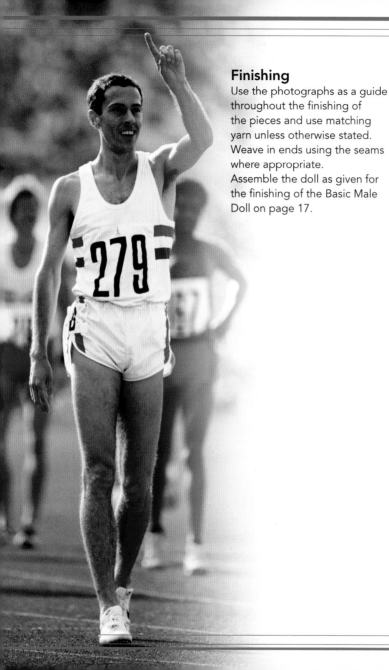

## Finishing

Use the photographs as a guide throughout the finishing of the pieces and use matching yarn unless otherwise stated. Weave in ends using the seams where appropriate.

Assemble the doll as given for the finishing of the Basic Male Doll on page 17.

### Head and face

Pin and stitch ears and hair to the head.

Embroider the face as follows:

Eyes: Using black yarn, work bullion knots (wrapped around needle 5 times).

Mouth: Using red embroidery thread, work in backstitch.

### Vest

Using mattress stitch or backstitch, sew the side edges of the two pieces together to create side seams and sew shoulder seams.

Using a short length of black yarn and backstitch, embroider a number on to the Number Panel, then pin and stitch it to the front of the Vest.

### Shorts

Using mattress stitch or backstitch, sew the side edges together to create the back leg seams.

Using white yarn, make twisted cord 30cm (12in) long and thread through the eyelets.

### Trainers

Fold the cast-off edge in half, then sew together the cast-off edge and back seam.

For laces, cut a length of white yarn, thread through the top of the trainers and tie into a bow.

# SEBASTIAN COE

**FACT**
Coe received
a knighthood in the
2006 New Year's
Honours List.

## Materials

### DOLL
>>> Patons Fab DK; 274m/100g
ball (100% acrylic):
1 ball in cream, 2307 (A)
>>> Patons Fab DK; 68m/25g
ball (100% acrylic):
1 ball in black, 2311 (B)
>>> Pair of 3.25mm (US 3)
knitting needles
>>> Stitch holder or safety pin
>>> Tapestry needle
>>> Toy stuffing
>>> Red embroidery thread
>>> Embroidery needle

### OUTFIT
>>> Patons Fab DK; 68m/25g
ball (100% acrylic):
1 ball in white, 2306 (C)
>>> Patons Diploma Gold DK;
120m/50g ball (55% wool,
25% acrylic, 20% nylon):
1 ball in navy, 6167 (D)
>>> Patons Fab DK; as above:
1 ball in red, 2306 (E)

## Pattern
### DOLL
Using A, make a Basic Male Doll
following the instructions on
page 16.

**FACT**
Coe retired from
competitive athletics
in 1990 and became
a Member of
Parliament.

## HAIR

Using B and 3.25mm (US 3) needles, cast on 13 sts.
Rows 1–6: Knit.
Row 7: K1, m1, knit to last st, m1, k1. (15 sts)
Row 8: Knit.
Row 9: Work as row 7. (17 sts)
Rows 10–20: Knit.
Row 21: K4, k2togtbl, k5, k2tog, k4. (15 sts)
Row 22: Knit.
Row 23: K4, k2togtbl, k3, k2tog, k4. (13 sts)
Row 24: Knit.
Row 25: K4, k2togtbl, k1, k2tog, k4. (11 sts)
Rows 26–28: Knit.
Row 29: K1, k2togtbl, k to last 3 sts, k2tog, k1. (9 sts)
Rows 30–33: Knit.
Cast off.

## VEST (MAKE 2)

Using C and 3.25mm (US 3) needles, cast on 20 sts.
Row 1: Knit.
Row 2: Knit.
Starting with a knit row, work 9 rows in stocking stitch.
Break off C, join in D.
Work 3 rows in stocking stitch.
Break off D, join in C.
Row 15: Purl.
Break off C, join in E.
Work 3 rows in stocking stitch.
Break off E, join in C.

Work 2 rows in stocking stitch.
Rows 21–22: Cast off 2 sts at beginning of row. (16 sts)
Row 23: Knit.
Row 24: Purl.
**Shape neck**
Row 25 (RS): K4, p1, transfer the rem 6 sts on to a stitch holder or safety pin. (5 sts)
Row 26: K1, p4.
Row 27: K2, k2tog, k1. (4 sts)
Row 28: K1, p3.
Row 29: K1, k2tog, k1. (3 sts)
Row 30: K1, p2.
Cast off.
Transfer stitches from stitch holder on to the needle and rejoin yarn.
Row 25: Cast off 6 sts, knit to end. (5 sts)
Row 26: P4, k1.
Row 27: K1, k2togtbl, k2. (4 sts)
Row 28: P3, k1.
Row 29: K1, k2togtbl, k1. (3 sts)
Row 30: P2, k1.
Cast off.

## NUMBER PANEL

Using D and 3.25mm (US 3) needles, cast on 10 sts.
Row 1: Knit.
Row 2: K1, p8, k1.
Repeat last 2 rows 3 times more.
Cast off.

## SHORTS

### Legs (make 2)

Using D and 3.25mm (US 3) needles, cast on 18 sts.
Row 1: Knit.
Row 2: Knit.
Starting with a knit row, work 6 rows in stocking stitch.
Transfer on to a stitch holder and make Leg 2.

### Join legs

Row 9: Knit 18 sts on Leg 1, knit across 18 sts on Leg 2. (36 sts)
Row 10: Purl.
Work 9 rows in stocking stitch.
Row 20: Knit
Row 21: K2 [k2tog, yfwd, k2] 4 times, k2, [k2tog, yfwd, k2] 3 times, k2tog, yfwd, k2.
Cast off knitwise.

## TRAINERS (MAKE 2)

Using C and 3.25mm (US 3) needles, cast on 17 sts.
Row 1: Purl.
Row 2: K1, m1, k6, m1, k3, m1, k6, m1, k1. (21 sts)
Row 3: Purl.
Row 4: K9, m1, k3, m1, k9. (23 sts)
Row 5: Purl.
**Shape toe**
Next row: K10, m1, k3, m1, k8, turn, do not work remaining sts on the left-hand needle.
Next row: Sl1, p20, turn.
Next row: Sl1, k8, m1, k3, m1, k7, turn.

Next row: Sl1, p18, turn.
Next row: Sl1, k7, m1, k3, m1,
    k6, turn.
Next row: Sl1, p16, turn.
Next row: Sl1, knit to end.
Next row: P12, p2tog, p1,
    p2tog, p12. (27 sts)
Cast off.

SEB COE
AND
STEVE OVETT

### FACT
Coe is Chair
of the London
Organising
Committee for the
2012 Olympic
Games.

## Finishing
Use the photographs as a guide
throughout the finishing of
the pieces and use matching
yarn unless otherwise stated.
Weave in ends using the seams
where appropriate.
Assemble the doll as given for
the finishing of the Basic Male
Doll on page 17.

**Head and face**
Pin and stitch hair to the head.
Embroider the face as follows.
Eyes: Using black yarn, work
bullion knots (wrapped around
needle 5 times).
Mouth: Using red embroidery
thread, work in backstitch.

**Vest**
Using mattress stitch or
backstitch, sew the side edges
of the two pieces together to
create side seams and sew
shoulder seams.
Using a short length of black
yarn and backstitch, embroider
a number on to the Number
Panel, then pin and stitch it to
the front of the Vest.

**Shorts**
Using mattress stitch or
backstitch, sew the side edges
together to create the back
leg seams.
Using white yarn, make twisted
cord 30cm (12in) long and
thread through the eyelets.

**Trainers**
Fold the cast-off edge in half,
then sew together the cast-off
edge and back seam.
For laces, cut a length of white
yarn and, using straight stitch,
embroider the top of the trainers.

# ZOLA BUDD

**FACT**
Budd trained
and raced
barefoot.

## Materials

### DOLL

》》》 Patons Fab DK; 274m/100g ball (100% acrylic): 1 ball in cream, 2307 (A)

》》》 Patons Diploma Gold DK; 120m/50g ball (55% wool, 25% acrylic, 20% nylon): 1 ball in beige, 6143 (B)

》》》 Pair of 3.25mm (US 3) knitting needles

》》》 Stitch holder or safety pin

》》》 Tapestry needle

》》》 Toy stuffing

》》》 One 2.75mm (C–2) crochet hook

》》》 Short length of black yarn

》》》 Red embroidery thread

》》》 Embroidery needle

### OUTFIT

》》》 Patons Fab DK; 68m/25g ball (100% acrylic): 1 ball in white, 2306 (C)

》》》 Patons Diploma Gold DK; as above: 1 ball in navy blue, 6167 (D)

》》》 Patons Fab DK; as above: 1 ball in red, 2306 (E)

》》》 Short length of black yarn

## Pattern

### DOLL

Using A, make a Basic Female Doll following the instructions on page 18.

### VEST (MAKE 2)

Using C and 3.25mm (US 3) needles, cast on 14 sts.
Row 1: Knit.
Row 2: Knit.
Starting with a knit row, work 4 rows in stocking stitch.
Row 7: K1, m1, knit to last st, m1, k1. (16 sts)
Break off C, join in D.
Work 3 rows in stocking stitch.
Break off D, join in C.
Row 11: Knit.
Break off C, join in E.
Work 3 rows in stocking stitch.
Break off E, join in C.
Work 2 rows in stocking stitch.
Rows 17–18: Cast off 2 sts at beg of row. (12 sts)
Row 19: Knit.
Row 20: Purl.
**Shape neck**
Next row: K4, transfer the rem 8 sts on to a stitch holder or safety pin. (4 sts)
Next row: K1, p2, k1.

Next row: K1, k2tog, k1.
Next row: K1, p1, k1.
Next row: K3.
Next row: K1, p1, k1.
Cast off.
Transfer stitches from stitch
    holder on to the needle and
    rejoin yarn.
Cast off 4 sts, knit to end. (4 sts)
Next row: K1, p2, k1.
Next row: K1, k2togtbl, k1.
Next row: K1, p1, k1.
Next row: K3.
Next row: K1, p1, k1.
Cast off.

**NUMBER PANEL**
Using C and 3.25mm (US 3)
needles, cast on 10 sts.
Row 1: Knit.
Row 2: K1, p8, k1.
Repeat last 2 rows 3 times more.
Cast off.

**SHORTS (MAKE 2)**
Using C and 3.25mm (US 3)
needles, cast on 14 sts.
Row 1 (WS): Purl.
Row 2: K1, m1, knit to last st,
    m1, k1. (16 sts)
Row 3: Purl.
Row 4: K1, m1, knit to last st,
    m1, k1. (18 sts)

**FACT**
Although a successful
athlete, Budd is most
famous for colliding with
Mary Decker in the
3000m at the 1984
Los Angeles
Olympics.

Starting with a purl row, work
  5 rows in stocking stitch.
Row 10: K1, k2togtbl, knit to last
  3 sts, k2tog, k1. (16 sts)
Row 11: Purl.
Row 12: Knit.
Cast off knitwise.

## Finishing

Use the photographs as a guide
throughout the finishing of
the pieces and use matching
yarn unless otherwise stated.
Weave in ends using the seams
where appropriate.
Assemble the doll as given for
the finishing of the Basic Female
Doll on page 19.

### Hair

Using yarn B, cut 18 lengths of
yarn 30cm (12in) long and
divide the lengths into 6
sections of 3 yarn lengths. To
create a centre parting, attach
the hair to the head along the
centre of the head by inserting a
crochet hook under a stitch,
folding a section of hair in half
and pulling it through the fabric
to form a loop, then pass the
cut ends of strands through the
loop and pull tight to form a
tassel. Twist each section of hair,
fold it up towards the crown and
stitch in place. Allow the loose
ends to poke through and form
short tufts.

### Face

Embroider the face as follows:
Eyes: Using black yarn, work
bullion knots (wrapped around
needle 5 times).
Mouth: Using red embroidery
thread, work in backstitch.

### Vest

Using mattress stitch or
backstitch, sew the side edges
of the two pieces together to
create side seams and sew
shoulder seams.
Using a short length of black
yarn and backstitch, embroider
a number on to the Number
Panel, then pin and stitch it to
the front of the Vest.

### Shorts

Using mattress stitch or
backstitch, sew the side seams,
then stitch the centre 2 stitches
on cast-on edge together to
create leg holes.

# FLORENCE GRIFFITH-JOYNER

## FACT FILE

**SPORT**
Athletics
(100m, 200m, 4 x 100m
relay, 4 x 400m relay)
**NICKNAME**
Flo-Jo
**DOB**
21 December, 1959
(D. 21 September, 1998)
**NATIONALITY**
American
**OLYMPIC MEDALS**
1 Silver (1984, Los Angeles);
3 Gold, 1 Silver
(1988, Seoul)

>>> Toy stuffing
>>> One 2.75mm (C–2)
crochet hook
>>> Short length of black yarn
>>> Red embroidery thread
>>> Embroidery needle

**OUTFIT**
>>> Patons Fab DK; 68m/25g
ball (100% acrylic):
1 ball in red, 2306 (C)
1 ball in white, 2306 (D)
>>> Small amount of
blue yarn
>>> Small amount of
yellow yarn

## Materials

**DOLL**
>>> Patons Fab DK; 274m/100g
ball (100% acrylic):
1 ball in brown, 2309 (A)
>>> Patons Fab DK; 68m/25g
ball (100% acrylic):
1 ball in black, 2311 (B)
>>> Pair of 3.25mm (US 3)
knitting needles
>>> Pair of 2.75mm (US 2)
knitting needles
>>> Tapestry needle

## Pattern

**DOLL**
Using A, make a Basic Female
Doll following the instructions
on page 18.

**LEOTARD (MAKE 2)**
Using C and 3.25mm (US 3)
needles, cast on 14 sts.
Row 1 (WS): Purl.
Row 2: K1, m1, knit to last st,
m1, k1. (16 sts)
Row 3: Purl.
Row 4: K1, m1, knit to last st,
m1, k1. (18 sts)
Work 5 rows in stocking stitch.

**FACT**
Flo-Jo still holds
the world record
for both the 100m
and 200m.

Row 10: K1, k2togtbl, knit to last 3 sts, k2tog, k1. (16 sts)

Row 11: Purl.

Row 12: K1, k2togtbl, knit to last 3 sts, k2tog, k1. (14 sts)

Work 5 rows in stocking stitch.

Row 18: K1, m1, knit to last st, m1, k1. (16 sts)

Row 19: Purl.

Repeat last 2 rows once more. (18 sts)

Work 2 rows in stocking stitch.

Next row: K1, k2togtbl, knit to last 3 sts, k2tog, k1. (16 sts)

Next row: Purl.

Repeat last 2 rows twice more. (12 sts)

Cast off.

## LEOTARD STRAPS (MAKE 2)

Using D and 3.25mm (US 3) needles, cast on 2 sts.

Work 10 rows in garter stitch.

Next row: K1, m1, k1. (3 sts)

Work 17 rows in garter stitch.

Next row: K2tog, k1. (2 sts)

Work 10 rows in garter stitch.

Cast off.

## LEOTARD BELT

Using D and 3.25mm (US 3) needles, cast on 28 sts.

Cast off knitwise.

## NUMBER PANEL

Using A and 3.25mm (US 3) needles, cast on 10 sts.

Row 1: Knit.

Row 2: K1, p8, k1.

Repeat last 2 rows 3 times more.

Cast off.

## TRAINERS (MAKE 2)

Using D and 3.25mm (US 3) needles, cast on 17 sts.

Row 1: Purl.

Row 2: K1, m1, k6, m1, k3, m1, k6, m1, k1. (21 sts)

Row 3: Purl.

Row 4: K9, m1, k3, m1, k9. (23 sts)

Row 5: Purl.

Shape toe

Next row: K10, m1, k3, m1, k8, turn, do not work remaining sts on the left-hand needle.

Next row: Sl1, p20, turn.

Next row: Sl1, k8, m1, k3, m1, k7, turn.

Next row: Sl1, p18, turn.

Next row: Sl1, k7, m1, k3, m1, k6, turn.

Next row: Sl1, p16, turn.

Next row: Sl1, knit to end.

Next row: P12, p2tog, p1, p2tog, p12. (27 sts)

Cast off.

# Finishing

Use the photographs as a guide throughout the finishing of the pieces and use matching yarn unless otherwise stated. Weave in ends using the seams where appropriate.

Assemble the doll as given for the finishing of the Basic Female Doll on page 19.

Hair

Using yarn B, cut 48 lengths of yarn 30cm (12in) long and divide the lengths into 16 sections of 3 yarn lengths. Attach the hair to the head along the top seam by inserting a crochet hook under a stitch, folding a section of hair in half and pulling it through the fabric to form a loop, then pass the cut ends of strands through the loop and pull tight to form a tassel. Attach two more lines of hair lengths, each slightly offset from the last, with one immediately behind the first, then, the other 1.5cm (⅝in) lower. Draw the hair back and stitch the hair in place by working a line of running stitch between the last two lines of hair lengths.

Face

Embroider the face as follows: Eyes: Using black yarn, work bullion knots (wrapped around needle 5 times).

Mouth: Using red embroidery
thread, work in backstitch.
**Larger finger nails (make 2)**
Using C and 2.75mm (US 2)
needles, cast on 5 sts.
Cast off knitwise.
Repeat using D and blue yarn.
**Smaller finger nails (make 2)**
Using yellow yarn and 2.75mm
(US 2) needles, cast on 4 sts.
Cast off knitwise.
Weave in one loose end, then
use the other to stitch on to
hands of the doll.
**Leotard**
Using mattress stitch or
backstitch, sew the side seams.
Pin and stitch the straps to front
and back. Dress the doll in the
leotard, then stitch the centre
2 stitches on cast-on edge
together to create leg holes.
Using a short length of red yarn
and backstitch, embroider a
number on to the Number
Panel, then pin and stitch it to
the front of the Leotard.
Place Belt around waist and sew
ends together.
**Trainers**
Fold cast-off edge in half, then
sew together the cast-off edge
and back seam.
For laces, cut a length of
white yarn, thread through
the top of the trainers and tie
into a bow.

**FACT**
Flo-Jo was denied a
place on the 1984 relay
team because officials
feared her long acrylic
nails were a danger
when passing the
baton.

# CARL LEWIS

## Materials

### DOLL

>>> Patons Fab DK; 274m/100g
ball (100% acrylic):
1 ball in brown, 2309 (A)
>>> Patons Fab DK; 68m/25g
ball (100% acrylic):
1 ball in black, 2311 (B)
>>> Pair of 3.25mm (US 3)
knitting needles
>>> Stitch holder or safety pin
>>> Tapestry needle
>>> Toy stuffing

### OUTFIT

>>> Patons Fab DK; 68m/25g
ball (100% acrylic):
1 ball in red, 2306 (D)
1 ball in white, 2306 (C)

## Pattern

### DOLL

Using A, make a Basic Male Doll
following the instructions on
page 16.

### HAIR

Using B and 3.25mm (US 3)
needles, cast on 6 sts.
Work 4 rows in garter stitch.
Cast on 4 sts at beginning of
next 2 rows. (14 sts)

Work 4 rows in garter stitch.
Cast off 2 sts at beginning of
next 2 rows. (10 sts)
Work 10 rows in garter stitch.
Row 23: K1, sl1, k2tog, psso, knit
to last 4 sts, k3tog, k1. (6 sts)
Cast off knitwise.

### VEST (MAKE 2)

Using C and 3.25mm (US 3)
needles, cast on 20 sts.
Row 1: Knit.
Row 2: Knit.
Starting with a knit row, work
20 rows in stocking stitch.
Rows 23–24: Cast off 2 sts at the
beginning of row. (16 sts)
Work 2 rows in stocking stitch.
Shape neck
Row 27 (RS): K4, p1, transfer the
rem 11 sts on to a stitch
holder or safety pin. (5 sts)
Row 28: K1, p4.
Row 29: K2, k2tog, k1. (4 sts)
Row 30: K1, p3.
Row 31: K1, k2tog, k1. (3 sts)
Row 32: K1, p2.
Cast off.
Transfer 11 sts from stitch holder
on to the needle and rejoin
yarn.
Row 27: Cast off 6 sts, knit to
end. (5 sts)

Row 28: P4, k1.
Row 29: K1, k2togtbl, k2. (4 sts)
Row 30: P3, k1.
Row 31: K1, k2togtbl, k1. (3 sts)
Row 32: P2, k1.
Cast off.

## NUMBER PANEL

Using D and 3.25mm (US 3)
needles, cast on 10 sts.
Row 1: Knit.
Row 2: K1, p8, k1.
Repeat last 2 rows 3 times
    more.
Cast off.

## SHORTS

**Legs (make 2)**
Using D and 3.25mm
(US 3) needles, cast on 18
sts.
Row 1: Knit.
Row 2: Knit.
Starting with a knit row, work
    6 rows in stocking stitch.
Transfer on to a stitch holder
    and make Leg 2.
**Join legs**
Row 9: Knit 18 sts on Leg 1, knit
    across 18 sts on Leg 2. (36 sts)
Row 10: Purl.
Work 9 rows in stocking stitch.
Row 20: Knit.
Row 21: K2, [k2tog, yfwd, k2]
    4 times, k2, [k2tog, yfwd, k2]
    3 times, k2tog, yfwd, k2.
Cast off knitwise.

**FACT**
Lewis' world
record for the long
jump, set in 1984,
is yet to be
beaten.

## TRAINERS (MAKE 2)

Using C and 3.25mm (US 3)
needles, cast on 17 sts.
Row 1: Purl.
Row 2: K1, m1, k6, m1, k3, m1,
    k6, m1, k1. (21 sts)
Row 3: Purl.
Row 4: K9, m1, k3, m1, k9. (23 sts)
Row 5: Purl.
**Shape toe**
Next row: K10, m1, k3, m1, k8,
    turn, do not work remaining
    sts on the left-hand needle.
Next row: Sl1, p20, turn.
Next row: Sl1, k8, m1, k3, m1,
    k7, turn.
Next row: Sl1, p18, turn.

Next row: Sl1, k7, m1, k3, m1,
    k6, turn.
Next row: Sl1, p16, turn.
Next row: Sl1, knit to end.
Next row: P12, p2tog, p1,
    p2tog, p12. (27 sts)
Cast off.

## Finishing

Use the photographs as a guide
throughout the finishing of
the pieces and use matching
yarn unless otherwise stated.

Weave in ends using the seams where appropriate.

Assemble the doll as given for the finishing of the Basic Male Doll on page 17.

**Head and face**

Pin and stitch hair and ears to the head.

Using black yarn, work French knots around the edge of the strip of hair and on top of the head to create the hairline.

Embroider the face as follows:

Eyes: Using black yarn, work bullion knots (wrapped around needle 5 times).

Mouth: Using black yarn, work one long straight stitch.

**Vest**

Using mattress stitch or backstitch, sew the doll's right shoulder seam.

Using yarn C and with right side facing, pick up sts along neck line using 3.25mm (US 3) needle as follows: 5 sts down front, neck, 7 sts across front 5 sts back up to shoulder seam, 5 sts back down, then 7 sts across back and 5 sts up to shoulder.

Cast off knitwise.

Using mattress stitch or backstitch, sew the left shoulder and neckband together and sew the side edges of the two pieces together to create side seams.

Using white yarn and backstitch,

embroider USA to front of vest. Using a short length of red yarn and backstitch, embroider a number on to the Number Panel, then pin and stitch it to the front of the Vest.

**Shorts**

Using mattress stitch or backstitch, sew the side edges together to create the back leg seams.

Using red yarn, make twisted cord 30cm (12in) long and thread through the eyelets.

**Trainers**

Fold the cast-off edge in half, then sew together the cast-off edge and back seam.

For laces, cut a length of red yarn, thread through the top of the trainers and tie into a bow.

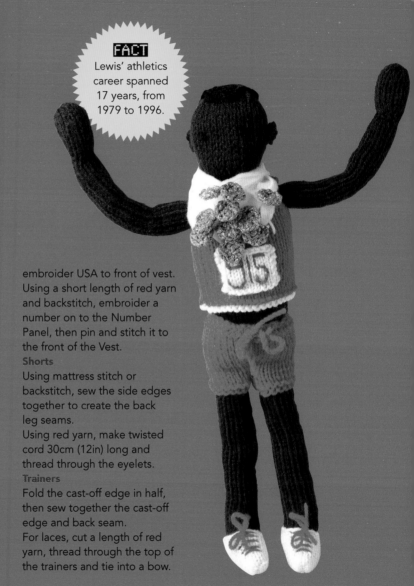

**FACT**

Lewis' athletics career spanned 17 years, from 1979 to 1996.

# CATHY FREEMAN

## Materials

### DOLL AND OUTFIT

》》》 Patons Fab DK; 68m/25g
ball (100% acrylic):
1 ball in green, 2319 (A)
1 ball in white, 2306 (B)
1 ball in brown, 2309 (C)
1 ball in yellow, 2305 (D)
1 ball in red, 2323 (E)

》》》 Adriafil Regina; 125m/50g
ball (100% wool):
1 ball in dark brown, 16 (F)

》》》 Pair of 3.25mm (US 3)
knitting needles

》》》 Tapestry needle

》》》 Toy stuffing

》》》 One 2.75mm
(C–2) crochet hook

》》》 Oddment of black yarn

》》》 Pink embroidery thread

》》》 Embroidery needle

## Pattern

### DOLL AND OUTFIT

Work the Basic Female Doll on
page 18, changing yarns as
directed.

### BODY AND HEAD

Using A and 3.25mm (US 3)
needles, work as for Basic
Female Doll until row 9.
Break off A, join in B.

Continue working from pattern
until row 33.
Break off B, join in A.
Work 2 rows in stocking stitch.
Break off A, join in C.
Work pattern to end.

### ARMS (MAKE 2)

Using A and 3.25mm (US 3)
needles, work Arm pattern until
row 28.
Break off A, join in C.
Work Arm pattern to end.

### LEGS (MAKE 2)

Using A and 3.25mm (US 3)
needles, work Leg pattern as for
Basic Female Doll until row 32.
Break off A, join in C.
Work Leg pattern to end.

### YELLOW STRIPE

Using D and 3.25mm (US 3)
needles, cast on 11 sts.
Work 8 rows in stocking stitch.
Next row: K5, transfer the rem
3 sts on to a stitch holder or
safety pin. (6 sts)
**Work 7 rows in stocking stitch.
Next row: K1, sl1, k2tog, psso,
k1. (3 sts)
Work 13 rows in stocking stitch.
Break off yarn and thread

through remain 3 sts on needle. Draw tight and secure the end. Transfer stitches from stitch holder and rejoin yarn.
Next row: K2tog, knit to end.
Work as given from ** to end of the pattern.

## HOOD
Using A and 3.25mm (US 3) needles, cast on 15 sts.
Row 1: Knit.
Row 2: K2, p11, k2.
Repeat last 2 rows 6 times more.
Row 15: K3, sl2 knitwise, k1, psso, knit to last 6 sts, sl2 knitwise, k1, psso, k3. (11 sts)
Row 16: K2, purl to last 2 sts, k2.
Row 17: Knit.
Row 18: Work as row 16.
Row 19: K2, sl2 knitwise, k1, psso, k1, sl2 knitwise, k1, psso, k2. (7 sts)
Row 20: K2, p3tog, k2. (5 sts)
Cast off knitwise.

## CENTRE HOOD STRIPE
Using B and 3.25mm (US 3) needles, cast on 4 sts.
Work 22 rows in garter stitch.
Cast off.

## NUMBER PANEL
Using B and 3.25mm (US 3) needles, cast on 10 sts.
Row 1: Knit.
Row 2: K1, p8, k1.

Repeat last 2 rows 3 times more.
Cast off.

## TRAINERS (MAKE 2)
Using E and 3.25mm (US 3) needles, cast on 17 sts.
Row 1: Purl.
Row 2: K1, m1, k6, m1, k3, m1, k6, m1, k1. (21 sts)
Row 3: Purl.
Break off E, join in D.
Row 4: K9, m1, k3, m1, k9. (23 sts)
Row 5: Purl.
**Shape toe**
Next row: K10, m1, k3, m1, k8, turn, do not work remaining sts on the left-hand needle.
Next row: Sl1, p20, turn.
Next row: Sl1, k8, m1, k3, m1, k7, turn.
Next row: Sl1, p18, turn.
Next row: Sl1, k7, m1, k3, m1, k6, turn.
Next row: Sl1, p16, turn.
Next row: Sl1, knit to end.
Next row: P12, p2tog, p1, p2tog, p12. (27 sts)
Cast off.

## Finishing
Use the photographs as a guide throughout the finishing of the pieces and use matching yarn unless otherwise stated. Weave in ends using the seams where appropriate.

Assemble the doll as given for
the finishing of the Basic Female
Doll on page 19.

**Hair**
Using yarn B, cut 18 lengths of
yarn 30cm (12in) long and divide
the lengths into 6 sections of
3 yarn lengths. Attach the hair
to the head along the top seam
by inserting a crochet hook
under a stitch, folding a section
of hair in half and pulling it
through the fabric to form a
loop, then pass the cut ends of
strands through the loop and
pull tight to form a tassel. Cut a
length of dark brown yarn, draw
the hair to the back of the head
and secure with a bow.

**Face**
Embroider the face as follows:
Eyes: Using black yarn, work
bullion knots (wrapped around
needle 5 times).
Mouth: Using pink embroidery
thread, work in backstitch.

**Outfit**
Using whip stitch, pin and sew
the Yellow stripe to the back of
the bottom and legs and the
Centre Hood strip to the Hood.
Attach the hood to the top of
the suit. Using a short length of
black yarn and backstitch,
embroider a number on to the
Number Panel, then pin and
stitch it to the front of the suit.

**Trainers**
Fold the cast-off edge in half,
then sew together the cast-off
edge and back seam.
For laces, cut a length of black
yarn, thread through the top of
the trainers and tie into a bow.

**FACT**
Freeman ran her
victory lap at the 2000
Sydney Games holding
both the Australian
and Aboriginal
flags.

**FACT**
Freeman is
famous for her
green and yellow
body suit.

# MICHAEL JOHNSON

## Materials
**DOLL**
>>> Patons Fab DK; 274m/100g
    ball (100% acrylic):
    1 ball in brown, 2309 (A)
>>> Patons Fab DK; 68m/25g
    ball (100% acrylic):
    1 ball in black, 2311 (B)
>>> Pair of 3.25mm (US 3)
    knitting needles
>>> Stitch holder or safety pin
>>> Tapestry needle
>>> Toy stuffing

**OUTFIT**
>>> Patons Diploma Gold DK;
    120m/50g ball (55% wool,
    25% acrylic, 20% nylon):
    1 ball in navy blue, 6167 (C)
>>> Patons Fab DK; 68m/25g
    ball (100% acrylic):
    1 ball in white, 2306 (D)
    1 ball in red, 2323 (E)
>>> Patons Diploma Gold DK as
    above;
    1 ball in gold, 6167 (F)
>>> Short amount of gold Lurex

## Pattern
**DOLL**
Using A, make a Basic Male Doll
following the instructions on
page 16.

### EARS (MAKE 2)
Using A and 3.25mm (US 3)
needles, cast on 6 sts.
Row 1: Knit.
Break off yarn and thread
through stitches on needle.
Draw tight and secure the end.

### HAIR
Using B and 3.25mm (US 3)
needles, cast on 4 sts.
Work 10 rows in garter stitch.
Next row: K1, m1, k2, m1, k1.
Continue working in garter
    stitch until the strip fits from
    top of head to back of neck.
Cast off.

### ALL-IN-ONE SUIT
**Legs (make 2)**
Using C and 3.25mm (US 3)
needles, cast on 20 sts.
Row 1: Knit.
Row 2: Purl.
Side stripes are worked using
    the intarsia technique. Keep
    the foll colour st patt correct
    throughout. Join in D.
Row 3: K7C, k6D, k7C.
Work 5 rows in stocking stitch.
Transfer on to a stitch holder
    and make Leg 2.
**Join legs**

Row 9: Knit 20 sts on Leg 1, knit across 20 sts on Leg 2. (40 sts)
Row 10: Purl.
Work 6 rows in stocking stitch.
Row 17: K7, k2tog, k2, k2togtbl, k14, k2togtbl, k2, k2tog, k7. (36 sts)
Work 3 rows in stocking stitch.
Row 21: K7, k2tog, k2togtbl, k14, k2togtbl, k2tog, k7. (32 sts)
Work 3 rows in stocking stitch.
Row 25: K8, m1, k2, m1, k16, m1, k2, m1, k8. (36 sts)
Work 9 rows in stocking stitch.
Row 35: K7, cast off 4 sts, k14 (include the last st from cast-off in the count), cast off 4 sts, k7 (include the last st from cast-off in the count).
Transfer the first 21 sts of the last row on to a stitch holder.

**Shape back right neck**
Work 2 rows in stocking stitch.
Row 38: Cast off 2 sts, purl to end. (5 sts)
Row 39: K1, k2tog, k1. (4 sts)
Row 40: P2tog, p2. (3 sts)
Row 41: Knit.
Row 42: Purl.
Cast off.

**Shape back left neck**
Transfer the group of 7 sts from stitch holder on to the needle and rejoin yarn with WS facing.
Work 2 rows in stocking stitch.

Row 38: Cast off 2 sts, purl to end. (5 sts)
Row 39: K1, k2togtbl, k1. (4 sts)
Row 40: P2togtbl, p2. (3 sts)
Row 41: Knit.
Row 42: Purl.
Cast off.

**Shape front neck**
Transfer 14 sts from stitch holder on to the needle and rejoin yarn with WS facing.
Work 2 rows in stocking stitch.
Next row: P5, cast off 4 sts, purl to end.
Transfer the first 5 sts of the last row on to a stitch holder.

**Shape front left neck**
Work as for Shape back right neck from row 39 to end.

**Shape front right neck**
Transfer stitches from stitch holder and rejoin yarn with RS facing. Work as for Shape back left neck from row 39 to end.

**MOTIF**
Using D and 3.25mm (US 3) needles, cast on 3 sts.
Row 1: Purl.
Row 2: K1, m1, k1, m1, k1. (5 sts)
Starting with a purl row, work 3 rows in stocking stitch.
Row 6: Sl1, k1, psso, k1, k2tog.
Row 7: Purl.
Cast off.

**FACT**
Johnson is the only male athlete in history to win both the 200m and 400m events at the same Olympics.

(69)

**TRAINERS (MAKE 2)**

Using G and 3.25mm (US 3) needles, cast on 17 sts.

Row 1: Purl.

Row 2: K1, m1, k6, m1, k3, m1, k6, m1, k1. (21 sts)

Row 3: Purl.

Row 4: K9, m1, k3, m1, k9. (23 sts)

Row 5: Purl.

**Shape toe**

Next row: K10, m1, k3, m1, k8, turn, do not work remaining sts on the left-hand needle.

Next row: Sl1, p20, turn.

Next row: Sl1, k8, m1, k3, m1, k7, turn.

Next row: Sl1, p18, turn.

Next row: Sl1, k7, m1, k3, m1, k6, turn.

Next row: Sl1, p16, turn.

Next row: Sl1, knit to end.

Next row: P12, p2tog, p1, p2tog, p12. (27 sts)

Cast off.

## Finishing

Use the photographs as a guide throughout the finishing of the pieces. Weave in ends. Assemble the doll as given for the finishing of the Basic Male Doll on page 17.

**Head and face**

Pin and stitch hair and ears to the head. Using black yarn, work French knots around the edge of the strip of hair and on top of the head to create the hairline. Embroider the face as follows:

Eyes: Using black yarn, work bullion knots (wrapped around needle 5 times).

Mouth: Using black yarn, work three straight stitches.

**All-in-one suit**

Using mattress stitch or backstitch, sew the side edges together to create the leg seams and a back seam.

Using backstitch, embroider a red line down either side of both white stripes.

Dress doll in the suit and sew shoulder seams.

Using backstitch, embroider USA on to the Motif, and sew on to the suit.

Using backstitch, embroider a number on to the Number Panel, then pin and stitch it to the front of the All-in-one suit.

**Trainers**

Fold the cast-off edge in half, then sew together the cast-off edge and back seam. Using red yarn and chain stitch, embroider a sloping L-shape on the outside of each trainer. For laces, using gold Lurex and straight stitch, embroider the top of the trainers.

**FACT**

Johnson's famous gold shoes were different sizes: the right was US size 11 and the left was US size 10.5, to fit Johnson's smaller left foot.

# HAILE GEBRSELASSIE

**FACT**
Gebrselassie ran
10km (6 miles) to
and from school
every day.

## Materials
**DOLL**
》》》 Patons Fab DK; 274m/100g
ball (100% acrylic):
1 ball in brown, 2309 (A)
》》》 Patons Fab DK; 68m/25g
ball (100% acrylic):
1 ball in black, 2311 (B)
》》》 Pair of 3.25mm (US 3)
knitting needles
》》》 Stitch holder or safety pin
》》》 Tapestry needle
》》》 Toy stuffing

**OUTFIT**
》》》 Patons Fab DK; as above:
1 ball in green, 2319 (C)
1 ball in white, 2306 (D)
1 ball in red, 2323 (E)

## Pattern
**DOLL**
Using A, make a Basic Male Doll
following the instructions on
page 16.

**EARS (MAKE 2)**
Using A and 3.25mm (US 3)
needles, cast on 6 sts.
Row 1: Knit.
Break off yarn and thread
through stitches on needle.
Draw tight and secure the end.

### HAIR

Using B and 3.25mm (US 3) needles, cast on 6 sts.
Work 4 rows in garter stitch.
Cast on 4 sts at beginning of next 2 rows. (14 sts)
Work 4 rows in garter stitch.
Cast off 2 sts at beginning of next 2 rows. (10 sts)
Work 10 rows in garter stitch.
Next row: K1, sl1, k2tog, psso, knit to last 4 sts, k3tog, k1. (6 sts)
Cast off knitwise.

### VEST (MAKE 2)

Using C and 3.25mm (US 3) needles, cast on 20 sts.
Row 1: Knit.
Row 2: Knit.
Starting with a knit row, work 20 rows in stocking stitch.
Rows 23–24: Cast off 2 sts at the beginning of row. (16 sts)
Work 2 rows in stocking stitch.
**Shape neck**
Row 27 (RS): K4, p1, transfer the rem 11 sts on to a stitch holder or safety pin. (5 sts)
Row 28: K1, p4.
Row 29: K2, k2tog, k1. (4 sts)
Row 30: K1, p3.
Row 31: K1, k2tog, k1. (3 sts)
Row 32: K1, p2.
Cast off.
Transfer 11 sts from stitch holder on to the needle, rejoin yarn.

Row 27: Cast off 6 sts, knit to end. (5 sts)
Row 28: P4, k1.
Row 29: K1, k2togtbl, k2. (4 sts)
Row 30: P3, k1.
Row 31: K1, k2togtbl, k1. (3 sts)
Row 32: P2, k1.
Cast off.

### NUMBER PANEL

Using D and 3.25mm (US 3) needles, cast on 10 sts.
Row 1: Knit.
Row 2: K1, p8, k1.
Repeat last 2 rows 3 times more.
Cast off.

### SHORTS

**Legs (make 2)**
Using E and 3.25mm (US 3) needles, cast on 18 sts.
Row 1: Knit.
Row 2: Knit.
Starting with a knit row, work 6 rows in stocking stitch.
Transfer on to a stitch holder and make Leg 2.
**Join legs**
Row 9: Knit 18 sts on Leg 1, knit across 18 sts on Leg 2. (36 sts)
Row 10: Purl.
Work 9 rows in stocking stitch.
Row 20: Knit.
Row 21: K2, [k2tog, yfwd, k2] 4 times, k2, [k2tog, yfwd, k2] 3 times, k2tog, yfwd, k2.
Cast off knitwise.

## TRAINERS (MAKE 2)

Using E and 3.25mm (US 3) needles, cast on 17 sts.

Row 1: Purl.

Row 2: K1, m1, k6, m1, k3, m1, k6, m1, k1. (21 sts)

Row 3: Purl.

Row 4: K9, m1, k3, m1, k9. (23 sts)

Row 5: Purl.

**Shape toe**

Next row: K10, m1, k3, m1, k8, turn, do not work remaining sts on the left-hand needle.

Next row: Sl1, p20, turn.

Next row: Sl1, k8, m1, k3, m1, k7, turn.

Next row: Sl1, p18, turn.

Next row: Sl1, k7, m1, k3, m1, k6, turn.

Next row: Sl1, p16, turn.

Next row: Sl1, knit to end.

Next row: P12, p2tog, p1, p2tog, p12. (27 sts)

Cast off.

# Finishing

Use the photographs as a guide throughout the finishing of the pieces and use matching yarn unless otherwise stated. Weave in ends using the seams where appropriate.

Assemble the doll as given for the finishing of the Basic Male Doll on page 17.

**Head and face**

Pin and stitch hair and ears to the head.

Embroider the face as follows:

Eyes: Using black yarn, work bullion knots (wrapped around needle 5 times).

Mouth: Using black yarn, work in backstitch.

**Vest**

Using mattress stitch or backstitch, sew the side edges of the two pieces together to create side seams and sew shoulder seams.

Using white yarn and backstitch, embroider the front of the vest.

Using black yarn and backstitch, embroider a number on to the Number Panel, then pin and stitch it to the front of the Vest.

**Shorts**

Using mattress stitch or backstitch, sew the side edges together to create the back leg seams.

Using red yarn, make twisted cord 30cm (12in) long and thread through the eyelets.

**Trainers**

Fold the cast-off edge in half, then sew together the cast-off edge and back seam.

Using green yarn and backstitch, embroider horizontal lines across each trainer.

For laces, using black yarn and straight stitch, embroider the top of the trainers.

# IAN THORPE

**FACT**
The fabric of
Ian Thorpe's made-to-
measure swimming suit
is based on that of
shark's skin.

## Materials

**DOLL AND OUTFIT**

>>> Patons Fab DK; 274m/100g
ball (100% acrylic):
1 ball in black, 2311 (A)
1 ball in cream, 2307 (B)
1 ball in yellow, 2305 (C)
>>> Pair of 3.25mm (US 3)
knitting needles
>>> Stitch holder or safety pin
>>> Tapestry needle
>>> Toy stuffing
>>> Red embroidery thread
>>> Embroidery needle
>>> Felt fabric ovals;
20 x 12mm (⅞ x ½in):
2 in pale blue

## Pattern

**DOLL AND OUTFIT**

Work the Basic Male Doll on
page 16, changing yarns as
directed.

**BODY AND HEAD**

Using A and 3.25mm (US 3)
needles, work as for Basic Male
Doll until row 37.
Break off A, join in B.
Complete the Basic Male Doll
Body pattern.

**ARMS**

Using A and 3.25mm (US 3)
needles, work as for Basic Male
Doll Arm pattern until row 33.
Break off A, join in B.
Complete the Basic Male Doll
Arm pattern.

## LEGS

Using A and 3.25mm (US 3) needles, work as for Basic Male Doll Leg pattern until Shape feet.

Break off A, join in B. Complete the Basic Male Doll Legs pattern.

## SWIMMING CAP

Using C and 3.25mm (US 3) needles, cast on 34 sts.

Row 1: Knit.

Row 2: Knit.

Starting with a knit row, work 6 rows in stocking stitch.

Row 9: K2, [K2tog, k2] 6 times. (26 sts)

Row 10: Purl.

Row 11: Knit.

Row 12: Purl.

Row 13: K1, [k2tog, k1] 8 times, k1. (18 sts)

Row 14: Purl.

Row 15: K1, [k2tog] 8 times, k1. (10 sts)

Row 16: Purl.

Break off yarn and thread through stitches on needle. Draw tight and secure the end.

## Finishing

Use the photographs as a guide throughout the finishing of the pieces and use matching yarn unless otherwise stated. Weave in ends using the seams where appropriate.

Assemble the doll as given for the finishing of the Basic Male Doll on page 17.

### Face

Embroider the face as follows:
Eyes: Using black yarn, work bullion knots (wrapped around needle 5 times).
Mouth: Using red embroidery thread, work in backstitch.

### Cap

Pin and stitch Cap to head.
Goggles: Attach felt ovals to a length of cream yarn, then pin and stitch to the cap.

**FACT**
Ian Thorpe has won more Olympic gold medals than any other Australian.

# CAROLINA KLUFT

## Materials

### DOLL

>>> Patons Fab DK; 274m/100g
ball (100% acrylic):
1 ball in cream, 2307 (A)

>>> Patons Fab DK; 68m/25g
ball (100% acrylic):
1 ball in pale yellow,
2330 (B)

>>> Pair of 3.25mm (US 3)
knitting needles

>>> Stitch holder or safety pin

>>> Tapestry needle

>>> Toy stuffing

>>> One 2.75mm (C–2)
crochet hook

>>> Red embroidery thread

>>> Embroidery needle

### OUTFIT

>>> Patons Fab DK; 68m/
25g ball (100% acrylic):
1 ball in yellow, 2305 (C)
1 ball in white, 2306 (D)
1 ball in royal blue, 2321 (E)

## Pattern

### DOLL

Using A, make a Basic Female
Doll following the instructions
on page 18.

### VEST (MAKE 2)

Using C and 3.25mm (US 3)
needles, cast on
14 sts.
Row 1: Knit.
Row 2: Knit.
Starting with a knit row, work 4
rows in stocking stitch.
Row 7: K1, m1, knit to last st,
m1, k1. (16 sts)
Starting with a purl row, work
9 rows in stocking stitch.

**FACT**
Kluft is the only athlete to have won three World titles in the heptathlon.

Rows 17–18: Cast off 2 sts at beg of row. (12 sts)
Row 19: Knit.
Row 20: Purl.
Shape neck
Next row: K4, transfer the rem 8 sts on to a stitch holder or safety pin. (4 sts)
Next row: K1, p2, k1.
Next row: K1, k2tog, k1.
Next row: K1, p1, k1.
Next row: K3.
Next row: K1, p1, k1.
Cast off.
Transfer stitches from stitch holder on to the needle and rejoin yarn.
Cast off 4 sts, knit to end. (4 sts)
Next row: K1, p2, k1.
Next row: K1, k2togtbl, k1.
Next row: K1, p1, k1.
Next row: K3.
Next row: K1, p1, k1.
Cast off.

**NUMBER PANEL**
Using D and 3.25mm (US 3) needles, cast on 10 sts.
Work 8 rows in stocking stitch.
Cast off.

**SHORTS (MAKE 2)**
Using E and 3.25mm (US 3) needles, cast on 14 sts.
Row 1 (WS): Purl.
Row 2: K1, m1, knit to last st, m1, k1. (16 sts)

Row 3: Purl.
Row 4: K1, m1, knit to last st,
    m1, k1. (18 sts)
Starting with a purl row, work
    5 rows in stocking stitch.
Row 10: K1, k2togtbl, knit to last
    3 sts, k2tog, k1. (16 sts)
Row 11: Purl.
Row 12: Knit.
Cast off knitwise.

## TRAINERS (MAKE 2)

Using A and 3.25mm (US 3)
needles, cast on 17 sts.
Row 1: Purl.
Row 2: K1, m1, k6, m1, k3, m1,
    k6, m1, k1. (21 sts)
Row 3: Purl.
Row 4: K9, m1, k3, m1, k9. (23 sts)
Row 5: Purl.
Shape toe
Next row: K10, m1, k3, m1, k8,
    turn, do not work remaining
    sts on the left-hand needle.
Next row: Sl1, p20, turn.
Next row: Sl1, k8, m1, k3, m1,
    k7, turn.
Next row: Sl1, p18, turn.
Next row: Sl1, k7, m1, k3, m1,
    k6, turn.
Next row: Sl1, p16, turn.
Next row: Sl1, knit to end.
Next row: P12, p2tog, p1,
    p2tog, p12. (27 sts)
Cast off.

## Finishing

Use the photographs as a guide
throughout the finishing of
the pieces and use matching
yarn unless otherwise stated.
Weave in ends using the seams
where appropriate.
Assemble the doll as given for
the finishing of the Basic Female
Doll on page 19.

Hair

Using yarn B, cut 18 lengths of
yarn 30cm (12in) long and divide
the lengths into 6 sections of
3 yarn lengths. Attach the hair
to the head along the top seam
by inserting a crochet hook
under a stitch, folding a section
of hair in half and pulling it
through the fabric to form a
loop, then pass the cut ends of
strands through the loop and
pull tight to form a tassel.
Attach one more line of hair
lengths, slightly offset and
immediately behind the first.
Draw the hair to the back of the
head and work a loose plait. To
secure the end of the plait, cut a
length of pale yellow yarn and
tie into a bow.

Head and face

Pin and stitch ears to the head.
Embroider the face as follows:
Eyes: Using black yarn, work
bullion knots (wrapped around
needle 5 times).

Mouth: Using red embroidery
thread, work in backstitch.

Vest

Using mattress stitch or
backstitch, sew the doll's right
shoulder seam.
Using yarn E and with right side
facing, pick up sts along neck
line using 3.25mm (US 3) needle
as follows: 5 sts down front neck,
7 sts across front, 5 sts back up
to shoulder seam, 5 sts back
down, then 7 sts across back
and 5 sts up to shoulder.
Cast off knitwise.
Using mattress stitch or
backstitch, sew the left shoulder
and neckband together and sew
the side edges of the two pieces
together to create side seams.
Using white yarn and backstitch,
embroider the front of the vest.
Using a short length of blue yarn
and backstitch, embroider a
number on to the Number
Panel, then pin and stitch it to
the front of the Vest.

Shorts

Using mattress stitch or
backstitch, sew the side and
back seams.

Trainers

Fold cast-off edge in half and
sew up, then sew up back seam.
For laces, using cream yarn and
straight stitch, embroider the
top of the trainers.

# CHRIS HOY

**FACT**
Hoy received a
knighthood
in 2009.

## Materials
### DOLL
>>> Patons Fab DK; 274m/100g
ball (100% acrylic):
1 ball in cream, 2307 (A)
>>> Patons Diploma Gold DK;
120m/50g ball (55% wool,
25% acrylic, 20% nylon):
1 ball in beige, 6143 (B)
>>> Pair of 3.25mm (US 3)
knitting needles
>>> Stitch holder or safety pin
>>> Tapestry needle
>>> Toy stuffing
>>> Short length of black yarn
>>> Pink embroidery thread
>>> Embroidery needle

### OUTFIT
>>> Patons Fab DK; 68m/25g
ball (100% acrylic):
1 ball in royal blue, 2321 (C)
1 ball in white, 2306 (D)
>>> Oddment of red yarn

## Pattern
### DOLL
Using A, make a Basic Male Doll
following the instructions on
page 16.

### HAIR
Using B and 3.25mm (US 3)
needles, cast on 6 sts.
Work 4 rows in garter stitch.
Cast on 4 sts at beginning of
next 2 rows. (14 sts)
Work 4 rows in garter stitch.
Cast off 2 sts at beginning of
next 2 rows. (10 sts)
Work 10 rows in garter stitch.
Next row: K1, sl1, k2tog, psso,
knit to last 4 sts, k3tog, k1.
(6 sts)
Cast off knitwise.

### ALL-IN-ONE SUIT
**Legs (make 2)**
Using C and 3.25mm (US 3)
needles, cast on 20 sts.
Row 1: Knit.
Row 2: Purl.
Work 6 rows in stocking stitch.
Transfer on to a stitch holder
and make Leg 2.
**Join legs**
Row 9: Knit 20 sts on Leg 1, knit
across 20 sts on Leg 2. (40 sts)
Row 10: Purl.
Work 6 rows in stocking stitch.
Row 17: K7, k2tog, k2, k2togtbl,
k14, k2togtbl, k2, k2tog, k7.
(36 sts)

Row 18: Purl.
Break off C, join in D.
Work 2 rows in stocking stitch.
Row 21: K7, k2tog, k2togtbl,
k14, k2togtbl, k2tog, k7.
(32 sts)
Work 3 rows in stocking stitch.
Row 25: K8, m1, k2, m1, k16,
m1, k2, m1, k8. (36 sts)
Work 5 rows in stocking stitch.
Row 31: K7, cast off 4 sts, k14
(include the last st from cast-
off in the count), cast off 4 sts,
k7 (include the last st from
cast-off in the count).
Transfer the first 21 sts of the
last row on to a stitch holder.

### Shape back right neck
Work 2 rows in stocking stitch.
Row 34: Cast off 2 sts, purl to
end. (5 sts)
Row 35: K1, k2tog, k1. (4 sts)
Row 36: P2tog, p2. (3 sts)
Row 37: Knit.
Row 38: Purl.
Cast off.

### Shape back left neck
Transfer the group of 7 sts from
stitch holder on to the needle
and rejoin yarn with WS facing.
Work 2 rows in stocking stitch.
Row 34: Cast off 2 sts, purl to
end. (5 sts)
Row 35: K1, k2togtbl, k1. (4 sts)
Row 36: P2togtbl, p2. (3 sts)
Row 37: Knit.
Row 38: Purl.

Cast off.
### Shape front neck
Transfer 14 sts from stitch holder
on to the needle and rejoin
yarn with WS facing.
Work 2 rows in stocking stitch.
Next row: P5, cast off 4 sts, purl
to end.
Transfer the first 5 sts of the last
row on to a stitch holder.

### Shape front left neck
Work as for Shape back right
neck from row 35 to end.
### Shape front right neck
Transfer stitch from stitch holder
on to the needle and rejoin
yarn with RS facing.
Work as for Shape back left
neck from row 35 to end.

### SLEEVES (MAKE 2)
Using C, and 3.25mm (US 3)
needles and with RS facing,
pick up 15 sts evenly along the
top of the armhole.
Starting with a purl row, work
33 rows in stocking stitch.

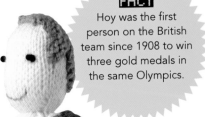

**FACT**
Hoy was the first
person on the British
team since 1908 to win
three gold medals in
the same Olympics.

Work 2 rows in garter stitch.
Cast off knitwise.

## SLEEVE STRIPES (MAKE 2)
Using C and 3.25mm (US 3) needles, cast on 3 sts.
Work 38 rows in garter stitch, or knit until the strip is the same length as the sleeve.
Cast off.

## TRAINERS (MAKE 2)
Using D and 3.25mm (US 3) needles, cast on 17 sts.
Row 1: Purl.
Row 2: K1, m1, k6, m1, k3, m1, k6, m1, k1. (21 sts)
Row 3: Purl.
Row 4: K9, m1, k3, m1, k9. (23 sts)
Row 5: Purl.

### Shape toe
Next row: K10, m1, k3, m1, k8, turn, do not work remaining sts on the left-hand needle.
Next row: Sl1, p20, turn.
Next row: Sl1, k8, m1, k3, m1, k7, turn.
Next row: Sl1, p18, turn.
Next row: Sl1, k7, m1, k3, m1, k6, turn.
Next row: Sl1, p16, turn.
Next row: Sl1, knit to end.
Next row: P12, p2tog, p1, p2tog, p12. (27 sts)
Cast off.

## Finishing
Use the photographs as a guide throughout the finishing of the pieces and use matching yarn unless otherwise stated. Weave in ends using the seams where appropriate.
Assemble the doll as given for the finishing of the Basic Male Doll on page 17.

### Head and face
Pin and stitch hair to the head. Embroider the face as follows:
Eyes: Using black yarn, work bullion knots (wrapped around needle 5 times).
Mouth: Using pink embroidery thread, work in backstitch.

### All-in-one suit
Using mattress stitch or backstitch, sew the doll's right shoulder seam.
Using yarn D and with right side facing, pick up sts along neck line using 3.25mm (US 3) needle as follows: 5 sts down front neck, 7 sts across front, 5 sts back up to shoulder seam, 5 sts back down, then 7 across back and 5 sts up to shoulder, leaving 3 sts at end for other shoulder.
Cast off knitwise.
Using mattress stitch or backstitch, sew the left shoulder and neckband together, then sew the side edges together to create side and back leg seams. Pin and stitch the Sleeve stripes down the centre of each sleeve. Using chain stitch and red yarn, embroider a line down both sides of the blue stripe.

### Trainers
Fold the cast-off edge in half, then sew together the cast-off edge and back seam.

FACT
Hoy was inspired to take up cycling at the age of six, after seeing the film E.T.

# USAIN BOLT

## Materials
### DOLL
>>> Patons Fab DK; 274m/100g
ball (100% acrylic):
1 ball in brown, 2309 (A)
>>> Patons Fab DK; 68m/25g
ball (100% acrylic):
1 ball in black, 2311 (B)
>>> Pair of 3.25mm (US 3)
knitting needles
>>> Stitch holder or safety pin
>>> Tapestry needle
>>> Toy stuffing
>>> Pink embroidery thread
>>> Embroidery needle

### OUTFIT
>>> Patons Fab DK; 68m/25g
ball (100% acrylic):
1 ball in yellow, 2305 (C)
1 ball in green, 2319 (D)
1 ball in white, 2306 (E)
>>> Gold embroidery thread

## Pattern
### DOLL
Using A, make a Basic Male Doll
following the instructions on
page 16.

### EARS (MAKE 2)
Using A and 3.25mm (US 3)
needles, cast on 6 sts.
Row 1: Knit.
Break off yarn and thread
through stitches on needle.
Draw tight and secure the end.

### VEST (MAKE 2)
Using C and 3.25mm (US 3)
needles, cast on 20 sts.
Row 1: Knit.
Row 2: Knit.
Starting with a knit row, work
20 rows in stocking stitch.
Rows 23–24: Cast off 2 sts at the
beginning of row. (16 sts)
Work 2 rows in stocking stitch.
**Shape neck**
Row 27 (RS): K4, p1, transfer the
rem 11 sts on to a stitch
holder or safety pin. (5 sts)

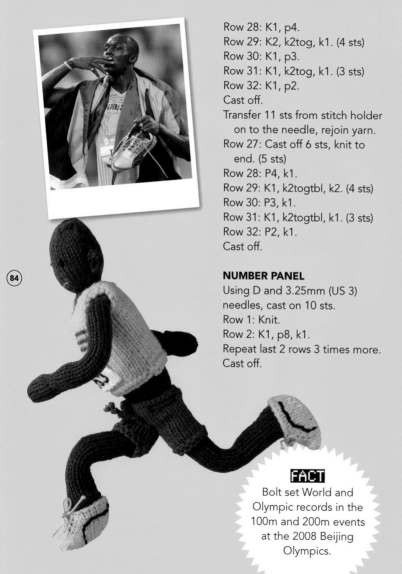

Row 28: K1, p4.
Row 29: K2, k2tog, k1. (4 sts)
Row 30: K1, p3.
Row 31: K1, k2tog, k1. (3 sts)
Row 32: K1, p2.
Cast off.
Transfer 11 sts from stitch holder on to the needle, rejoin yarn.
Row 27: Cast off 6 sts, knit to end. (5 sts)
Row 28: P4, k1.
Row 29: K1, k2togtbl, k2. (4 sts)
Row 30: P3, k1.
Row 31: K1, k2togtbl, k1. (3 sts)
Row 32: P2, k1.
Cast off.

## NUMBER PANEL

Using D and 3.25mm (US 3) needles, cast on 10 sts.
Row 1: Knit.
Row 2: K1, p8, k1.
Repeat last 2 rows 3 times more.
Cast off.

FACT
Bolt set World and Olympic records in the 100m and 200m events at the 2008 Beijing Olympics.

## SHORTS

**Legs (make 2)**
Using E and 3.25mm (US 3) needles, cast on 18 sts.
Row 1: Knit.
Row 2: Knit.
Starting with a knit row, work 6 rows in stocking stitch.
Transfer on to a stitch holder and make Leg 2.

**Join legs**
Row 9: Knit 18 sts on Leg 1, knit across 18 sts on Leg 2. (36 sts)
Row 10: Purl.
Work 9 rows in stocking stitch.
Row 20: Knit.
Row 21: K2, [k2tog, yfwd, k2] 4 times, k2, [k2tog, yfwd, k2] 3 times, k2tog, yfwd, k2.
Cast off knitwise.

## TRAINERS (MAKE 2)

Using E and 3.25mm (US 3) needles, cast on 17 sts.
Row 1: Purl.
Row 2: K1, m1, k6, m1, k3, m1, k6, m1, k1. (21 sts)
Row 3: Purl.
Row 4: K9, m1, k3, m1, k9. (23 sts)
Row 5: Purl.

**Shape toe**
Next row: K10, m1, k3, m1, k8, turn, do not work remaining sts on the left-hand needle.
Next row: Sl1, p20, turn.
Next row: Sl1, k8, m1, k3, m1, k7, turn.

Next row: Sl1, p18, turn.
Next row: Sl1, k7, m1, k3, m1,
  k6, turn.
Next row: Sl1, p16, turn.
Next row: Sl1, knit to end.
Next row: P12, p2tog, p1,
  p2tog, p12. (27 sts)
Cast off.

## Finishing

Use the photographs as a guide
throughout the finishing of
the pieces and use matching
yarn unless otherwise stated.
Weave in ends using the seams
where appropriate.
Assemble the doll as given for
the finishing of the Basic Male
Doll on page 17.

**Head and face**

Pin and stitch ears to the head.
Embroider the face as follows:
Eyes: Using black yarn, work
bullion knots (wrapped around
needle 5 times).
Mouth: Using pink embroidery
thread, work in backstitch.

**Vest**

Using mattress stitch or
backstitch, sew the side edges
of the two pieces together to
create side seams and sew
shoulder seams.
Using green yarn and backstitch,
embroider the front of the vest.
Using black yarn and backstitch,
embroider a number on to the

Number Panel, then pin and
stitch it to the front of the Vest.

**Shorts**

Using mattress stitch or
backstitch, sew the side edges
together to create the back
leg seams.
Using green yarn, make twisted
cord 30cm (12in) long and
thread through the eyelets.

**Trainers**

Fold the cast-off edge in half,
then sew together the cast-off
edge and back seam.
Using black yarn and backstitch,
embroider curved lines across
each trainer.
For laces, cut a length of gold
emboidery thread, thread
through the top of the trainers
and tie into a bow.

**FACT**
Bolt is famous
for his 'To Di
World' victory
pose.

85

# TRAIN TO BE KNIT-FIT!

**The following steps provide you with everything you need to create your own knitted sports star. It's easier than you think!**

## Working from a pattern

Before starting any pattern, always read it through. This will give you an idea of how the design is structured and the techniques that are involved. Each pattern includes the following basic elements:

### MATERIALS

This section gives a list of materials required, including the amount of yarn, the sizes of needles and any extras. The yarn amounts specified are based on average requirements and are therefore approximate.

### ABBREVIATIONS

Knitting instructions are normally given in an abbreviated form, which saves valuable space. In this book the most commonly used abbreviations are listed on page 96.

### PROJECT INSTRUCTIONS

Before starting to knit, read the instructions carefully to understand the abbreviations used, how the design is structured and in which order each piece is worked. However, there may be some parts of the pattern that only become clear when you are knitting them.

Asterisks or brackets are used to indicate the repetition of a sequence of stitches. For example: *k3, p1; rep from * to end. This means, knit three stitches, then purl one stitch, then repeat this sequence to the end of the row. It could also be written: [k3, p1] to end. Asterisks and brackets may be used together in a row. For example: *k4, p1, [k1, p1] 3 times; rep from * to end. The part of the instruction in brackets indicates that these stitches only are to be repeated three times before returning to the instructions immediately after the asterisk.

When repeating anything, make sure that you are doing so the correct number of times. For example: [k1, p1] twice means that 4 stitches are worked, but *k1, p1; rep from * twice more means 6 stitches are worked.

When you put your knitting aside, always mark where you are on the pattern; it is better to be safe than sorry, especially if a complex stitch is involved.

## TENSION AND SELECTING CORRECT NEEDLE SIZE

Tension can differ quite dramatically between knitters. This is because of the way that the needles and the yarn are held. So if your tension does not match that stated in the pattern, you should change your needle size following this simple rule:

>>> If your knitting is too loose, your tension will read that you have fewer stitches and rows than the given tension, and you will need to change to a thinner needle, or a smaller needle size, to make the stitch size smaller.

>>> If your knitting is too tight, your tension will read that you have more stitches and rows than the given tension, and you will need to change to a thicker needle, or a larger needle size, to make the stitch size bigger.

## FINISHING

The Finishing section in each project will tell you how to join the knitted pieces together. Always follow the recommended sequence.

**KNITTING TIP**
Always take the time to check your tension – it ensures the accuracy of your knitting!

# Making a slip knot

A slip knot is the basis of all casting-on techniques and is therefore the starting point for almost everything you do in knitting.

1   Wind the yarn around two fingers twice, as shown. Insert a knitting needle through the first (front) strand and under the second (back) one.

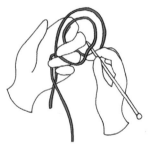

2   Using the needle, pull the back strand through the front one to form a loop. Holding the loose ends of the yarn with your left hand, pull the needle upwards, thus tightening the knot.

## Casting on

Casting on is the term used for making a row of stitches to be used as a foundation for your knitting.

1   Place the slip knot on the needle, leaving a long tail, and hold the needle in your right hand.

2   *Wind the loose end of the yarn around your thumb from front to back. Place the ball end of the yarn over your left forefinger.

3   Insert the point of the needle under the loop on your thumb. With your right index finger, take the ball end of the yarn over the point of the needle.

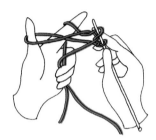

4   Pull a loop through to form the first stitch. Remove your left thumb from the yarn. Pull the loose end to secure the stitch. Repeat from * until the required number of stitches has been cast on.

## The basic stitches

The knit and purl stitches form the basis of all knitted fabrics.

### KNIT STITCH (K)

1   Hold the needle with the cast-on stitches in your left hand, with the loose yarn at the back of the work. Insert the right-hand needle from left to right through the front of the first stitch on the left-hand needle. Wrap the yarn from left to right over the point of the right-hand needle.

2   Draw the yarn through the stitch, thus forming a new stitch on the right-hand needle. Slip the original stitch off the left-hand needle. To knit a row, repeat until all the stitches have been transferred from the left-hand needle.

### PURL STITCH (P)

1   Hold the needle with the stitches in your left hand, with the loose yarn at the front of the work. Insert the right-hand needle from right to left into the front of the first stitch on the left-hand needle. Wrap the yarn from right to left, up and over the point of the right-hand needle.

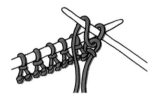

2   Draw the yarn through the stitch, thus forming a new stitch on the right-hand needle. Slip the original stitch off the left-hand needle, keeping the new stitch on the right-hand needle. To purl a row, repeat until all the stitches have been transferred from the left-hand needle to the right-hand needle.

### KNIT THROUGH THE BACK OF LOOP (KTBL)

Work as for a knit stitch but insert the right-hand needle from left to right through the back of the first stitch on the left-hand needle.

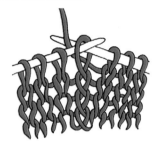

### PURL THROUGH THE BACK OF LOOP (PTBL)

Work as a purl stitch but insert the right-hand needle from left to right through the back of the first stitch on the left-hand needle.

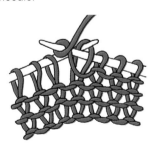

### SLIP STITCH (SL)

Following the stitch pattern set, insert the right-hand needle into the first stitch on the left-hand needle as if to knit or purl. Transfer it on to the right-hand needle without wrapping the yarn around the right-hand needle to make a new stitch.

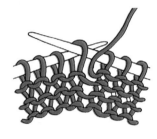

## Shaping

This is achieved by increasing or decreasing the number of stitches you are working.

### INCREASING (INC)

The simplest method of increasing one stitch is to create two stitches out of one stitch. Work a stitch into the front of the stitch to be increased into; then, before slipping it off the needle, place the right-hand needle behind the left-hand one and work again into the back of it. Slip the original stitch off the left-hand needle.

### MAKING A STITCH (M1)

Another form of increasing involves working into the strand between two stitches.

1    Insert the right-hand needle from front to back under the horizontal strand that runs between the stitches on the right- and left-hand needles.

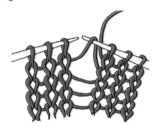

2    Insert the left-hand needle under the strand from front to back, twisting it as shown, to prevent a hole from forming, and knit (or purl) through the back of the loop. Slip the new stitch off the left-hand needle.

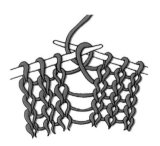

### MAKING A YARN FORWARD (YFWD)

A yarn forward is a loop of yarn placed over the right-hand needle that is worked on following rows like any other stitch and creates a hole in the knitted fabric. Work to the position of the yarn forward and bring the yarn forward (towards you) between the tips of the needles. Then take the yarn backward (away from you) over the right-hand needle and knit the next stitch.

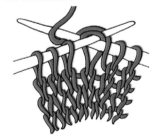

## DECREASING (K2TOG, K2TOGTBL, P2TOG, P2TOGTBL)

The simplest method of decreasing one stitch is to work two stitches together.

To knit two stitches together (k2tog), insert the right-hand needle from left to right through the front of the second stitch and then first stitch nearest the tip of the left-hand needle and knit them together as one stitch.

To knit two together through the back of the loops (k2togtbl), insert the right-hand needle from right to left through the back of the first and then second stitch nearest the tip of the left-hand needle and knit them together as one stitch.

To purl two stitches together (p2tog), insert the right-hand needle from right to left through the front of the first and then second stitch nearest the tip of the left-hand needle, then purl them together as one stitch.

To purl two together through the back of the loops (p2togtbl), insert the right-hand needle from left to right through the back of the second and then first stitch nearest the tip of the needle and purl them together as one stitch.

## Intarsia

This technique creates a single thickness fabric with more than one colour worked on each row. The fabric becomes a series of linked blocks of colour, each block with its own length of yarn. To begin, work as directed until the first colour change. Join in the new colour by holding the tail of the new yarn in the palm of the left hand, laying the new yarn over the old colour from left to right and then taking the new yarn behind the old colour to knit the next stitch. Release the tail of the new yarn and gently pull on it to adjust the size of the first stitch. Continue in this fashion, across the first row, joining in a new length of yarn for each new colour block. On the following rows, work the row as directed until the first colour change and then, to avoid a hole in the fabric, the blocks are linked before the next block of colour is worked. To link the blocks, lay the old colour over the new colour, drop the old colour, pick up the new colour and, with the yarn from the old colour looped over the new colour, work the next stitch. Continue linking the blocks at each colour change until the block is completed.

## Casting off

This is the most commonly used method of securing stitches once you have finished a piece of knitting. The cast-off edge should have the same 'give' or elasticity as the fabric, and you should cast off in the stitch used for the main fabric unless the pattern directs otherwise.

### KNITWISE

Knit two stitches. *Using the point of the left-hand needle, lift the first stitch on the right-hand needle over the second, then drop it off the needle. Knit the next stitch and repeat from * until all stitches have been worked off the left-hand needle and only one stitch remains on the right-hand needle. Cut the yarn, leaving enough to sew in the end, thread the end through the stitch, then slip it off the needle. Draw the yarn up firmly to fasten off.

### PURLWISE

Work as for knitwise but purl the stitches rather than knit them.

# GET SET, SEW!

## Finishing techniques

You may have finished knitting but there is one crucial step still to come, the sewing up of the seams. It is tempting to start this as soon as you cast off the last stitch but a word of caution, make sure that you have good light and plenty of time to complete the task.

## MATTRESS STITCH (SIDE EDGES)

This stitch makes an almost invisible seam on the knit side of stocking stitch. Thread a tapestry needle with yarn and position the pieces side by side, right sides facing.

1    Working from the bottom of the seam to the top, come up from back to front at the base of the seam, to the left of the first stitch in from the edge, on the left-hand side and leave a 10cm (4in) tail of yarn. Take the needle across to the right-hand piece, to the right of the first stitch and pass the needle under the first two of the horizontal bars that divide the columns of stitches above the cast-on.

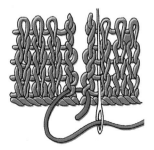

2    Take the needle across to the left-hand piece, insert the needle down where it last emerged on the left-hand edge and pass the needle under two of the horizontal bars that divide the columns of stitches. Take the needle across to the right-hand piece, insert the needle down through the fabric where it last emerged on the right-hand edge and pass the needle under the first two of the horizontal bars that divide the columns of stitches above the cast-on. Repeat step 2 until the seam has been closed.

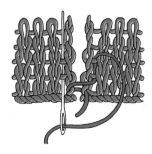

### MATTRESS STITCH
### (TOP AND BOTTOM EDGES)

Thread a tapestry needle with yarn and position the pieces top and bottom, right sides facing outermost. Working right to left, come up from back to front through the centre of the first stitch on the right edge of the seam. Take the needle to across the top piece, pass the needle under the two loops of the stitch above, then go down again, through the fabric, where the needle emerged on the lower piece. Repeat with the next stitch to the left.

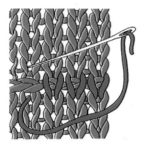

### WHIP STITCH

Thread a tapestry needle with yarn and position the pieces right sides together with the edge to be worked at the top. Working right to left and always from back to front pass the needle through the outermost strands of the edge fabric.

### INSERTING STUFFING

As with all soft toys, how you stuff your doll will directly affect the finished appearance. Stuff firmly, but do not stretch the knitting. Always stuff the extremities, such as the legs and arms, first and mould into shape as you go along. The amount of stuffing needed for each doll depends on the knitting tension and individual taste.

### BONDAWEB

This is a double-sided sheet adhesive that uses heat to bond flat surfaces together. It is useful for fabrics because it is washable and prevents fraying. Check the instructions on the packaging, then cut the Bondaweb to size, position it carefully, paper-side up, on to the knitted fabric as directed. If the fabric is quite thin then place a cloth underneath and another cloth on top, to protect the iron. Press gently with a hot iron. Remove the paper backing, place the second fabric on top of the Bondaweb and again, use a cloth and an iron to apply heat to the second fabric. The three layers are now permanently bonded. Bondaweb is washable in temperatures up to about 60 degrees centigrade.

## Adding detail

Embroidery and simple craft techniques have been used to add detail to the dolls.

### OUTLINING A DESIGN

Before adding embroidery to a fabric, it is sometimes useful to plan or outline where the stitches will go. Glass-headed pins can be used to mark the position of eyes or straight lines. For curved lines, an air-soluble pen can be used to mark the knitted fabric. Start with a light, thin line and then thicken the line when you are confident of its position. Do not ponder your decision for too long because most pens produce a mark that will fade within 24 hours. Avoid water-soluble pens as the marks these produce will only dissolve in water.

### BULLION KNOTS

To work a bullion knot, come up slightly to one side of the centre of the stitch, wrap the thread around the needle anticlockwise the number of times specified, then go down a short distance to the other side of the centre of the stitch.

## FRENCH KNOTS

1 Come up at point A (at which the stitch will sit), wrap the thread twice around the needle in an anticlockwise direction.

2 Push the wraps together and slide to the end of the needle. Go down close to the start point (A), pulling the thread through to form a knot.

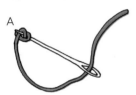

## CHAIN STITCH

Working from right to left, come up at the start of the line of stitching, insert the needle back through the fabric at the point it emerged and make a straight stitch emerging slightly to the left. Loop the working yarn under the tip of the needle and gently pull the needle through to create a loop on the surface of the fabric. Repeat as necessary, keeping the stitches even.

## RUNNING STITCH

Working from right to left, come up at the start of the line of stitching (A), go down at B and then come up at C. Do not pull the thread through the fabric. Go down at D and come up at E. Pull the thread through gently to create a dashed line of straight stitches. Repeat as necessary, keeping the stitches even.

## BACKSTITCH

Working from right to left, come up slightly to the left of the start of the line of stitching (A), go down at B and then come up at C. Pull the thread through. Go down again at B to make a backstitch, then come up at D, ready for the next stitch and then continue to create a solid line of short straight stitches.

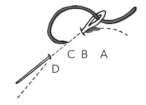

## SWISS DARNING OR DUPLICATE STITCH

This embroidery stitch duplicates the appearance of a knit stitch by following the passage of the yarn through the fabric.

Come up at the base of the stitch, then pass the needle under the two loops of the stitch above, and then go down again at the point the needle emerged. Repeat with the next stitch to either the left of or above of the last stitch.

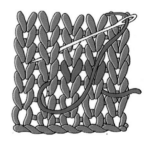

## SATIN STITCH

Work a series of short straight stitches, parallel to each other, to create a pad of stitches.

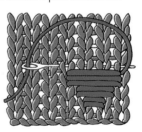

## TASSELS

Cut yarn to length as directed and group into individual tassel bundles. Insert a crochet hook through the fabric at the point from which you wish the tassel to hang, fold the yarn lengths for one tassel in half, loop the centre of the bundle around the hook and pull it through the fabric, then pass the cut ends of strands through the loop and gently pull tight to form a tassel. Trim the ends when all the tassels have been placed.

## PLAITS

Divide the strands into three sections – left, middle and right. *Cross the right section over the middle section and rearrange the sections so that the right section is now the middle section. Then cross the left section over the new middle section and again, rearrange the sections. Repeat from *, moving alternate right and left sections over the new middle sections until the sections are too short to cross into the middle. Secure the plait with a length of yarn or ribbon tied around the ends. Trim the ends. The plaits in this book are quite loose and the sections have not been pulled tight after each move.

# TEMPLATES

95

# ABBREVIATIONS

| | | | | | | |
|---|---|---|---|---|---|---|
| beg | beginning | mm | millimetre(s) | st st | stocking stitch |
| CC | contrast colour | MC | main colour | st(s) | stitch(es) |
| cm | centimetre | p | purl | tbl | through the back of loop |
| foll | follow (s)(ing) | p2tog | purl two together | tog | together |
| g | gram(s) | p3tog | purl three together | WS | wrong side |
| in | inch(es) | patt | pattern | yfwd | yarn forward |
| inc | increase | rem | remaining | [ ] | work directions within |
| k | knit | pso | pass stitch over | | square brackets as |
| k2tog | knit two together | psso | pass slipped stitch over | | directed |
| k3tog | knit three together | rep | repeat | * | work instructions after |
| m | metre | RS | right side | | asterisk as directed. |
| m1 | make one | sl | slip | | |

# AUTHOR THANKS

I would like to thank everybody for their help and support in creating this fantastic book. In particular, my knitters, Sandra Youngson, Eleanor Crombie and Elaine Low, for their quick turnaround and pattern checking skills! And, my ever so patient and loving partner Andy Daly, for supplying me with constant care and attention throughout. Thank you – I couldn't have done this without you all!

# PICTURE CREDITS

Project photography by Holly Jolliffe (www.hollyjolliffe.co.uk).
Thanks to Getty Images (www.gettyimages.com) for all photographic images of sporting events.

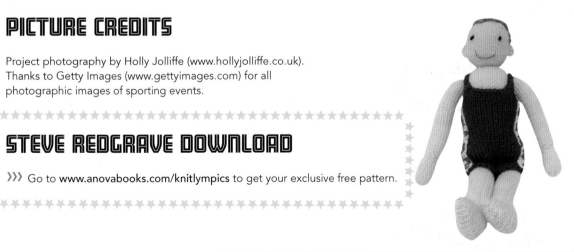

# STEVE REDGRAVE DOWNLOAD

>>> Go to www.anovabooks.com/knitlympics to get your exclusive free pattern.